HARRIET
BEECHER
STOWE

OTHER BOOKS BY SUZANNE M. COIL

FLORIDA

GEORGE WASHINGTON CARVER

POISONOUS PLANTS

THE POOR IN AMERICA

ROBERT HUTCHINGS GODDARD

HARRIET
BEECHER
·STOWE·

SUZANNE M. COIL

AN IMPACT BIOGRAPHY

FRANKLIN WATTS
NEW YORK·CHICAGO·LONDON·TORONTO·SYDNEY

FOR MY DEAR SISTERS
ETHEL AND HILDY
WITH LOVE

Photographs copyright © : The Bettmann Archive: pp. 1, 5, 6, 8 bottom, 12, 14, 15, 16; New York Public Library, Picture Collection: pp. 2, 3, 4, 7, 9, 10, 11, 13; North Wind Picture Archives, Alfred, ME: p. 8 top.

Library of Congress Cataloging-in-Publication Data

Coil, Suzanne M.
Harriet Beecher Stowe / Suzanne M. Coil.
p.   cm. — (An Impact biography)
Includes bibliographical references and index.
Summary: A biography of the nineteenth-century author whose anti-slavery novel "Uncle Tom's Cabin" helped intensify the disagreement between North and South.
ISBN 0-531-13006-1
1. Stowe, Harriet Beecher, 1811–1896—Biography—Juvenile literature.   2. Authors, American—19th century—Biography—Juvenile literature.   3. Abolitionists—United States—Biography—Juvenile literature.   [1. Stowe, Harriet Beecher, 1811–1896.   2. Authors, American.]   I. Title.
PS2956.C59   1993
813'.3—dc20
[B]   93-13710 CIP AC

CONTENTS

HARRIET BEECHER STOWE
by Paul Laurence Dunbar

She told the story, and the whole world wept
  At wrongs and cruelties it had not known
  But for this fearless woman's voice alone.
  She spoke to consciences that long had slept.

Her message, Freedom's clear reveille, swept
  From heedless hovel to complacent throne.
  Command and prophecy were in the tone,
  And from its sheath the sword of justice leapt.

Around two peoples swelled a fiery wave,
  But both came forth transfigured from the flame.
  Blest be the hand that dared be strong to save,

And blest be she who in our weakness came—
  Prophet and priestess! At one stroke she gave
  A race to freedom, and herself to fame.

From *The Century Magazine*,
November 1898

PREFACE

ON JANUARY 1, 1811, Americans congratulated one another on the birth of a new year. That year, they would celebrate the thirty-fifth anniversary of the signing of the Declaration of Independence. Although their young, growing nation was still struggling to define its character and its place in the world, they could nevertheless point with pride to the progress they had made since the hard-fought Revolution had freed them from the domination of England.

Much had happened in the intervening years. The same spirit that had inspired the original colonists to cross the ocean to settle in the New World had sent their children pouring over the Appalachian Mountains to conquer the territories to the west. The Union now comprised seventeen states: Vermont, Ohio, Kentucky, and Tennessee having been added to the original thirteen. The purchase of the Lousiana Territory in 1803 had extended the western limits of the country all the way to the Rocky Mountains, and explorers, trappers, and settlers were sending back colorful tales of the rich, fabled lands beyond the Mississippi. Raw, rough, and wild, the young country was growing and prospering. It was exciting to be an American; everything seemed possible. The future gleamed like gold across the horizon.

But not all Americans were pleased with the state of the Union. The practice of slavery, inherited from English colonial times, had taken root and spread like an ugly weed across the nation. For a while, people believed that slavery would gradually disappear. But as the nation extended its boundaries, the need for labor grew—and so did slavery.

Some Americans, known as abolitionists, believed that slavery should be condemned. They argued that not only was slavery against God's laws but that it contradicted the ideals of freedom and equality for which the Revolution had been fought. They agitated so much that a law forbidding the further importation of slaves was passed by Congress in 1807. But the law was having little effect. Great numbers of slaves were still being smuggled into the country to fill the ever-growing need for labor on the thriving southern plantations. Little was being done to stop the illegal trade or to punish the lawbreakers.

Outraged by the situation, the abolitionist movement set about enlisting new members. Slavery was morally wrong, the abolitionists said. Surely, God would punish a nation that permitted human beings to be bought and sold. He would bring down his wrath on those who allowed fellow humans to suffer in bondage.

In the years to come, the question of slavery would fester and grow like a deadly malignancy threatening the life of the nation until only radical surgery, in the form of a tragic civil war, could cure the nation of its disease. But now, in 1811, something happened that seemed like an omen of the future.

One night, settlers in New Madrid, a little town on the banks of the Mississippi in the Missouri Territory, were flung from their beds as the most severe earthquake ever to hit the nation began to rumble and roar and tear the earth apart. With an intensity of 10, the highest point on the earthquake measurement scale, the roaring grew until it shook the land over a million-square-mile area.

For hundreds of miles around New Madrid, the earth

churned, spewing up rocks and trees, sinking and rising in frightening undulations like a vast ocean. The mighty Ohio and Mississippi rivers ran backward in their courses. In the young cities of St. Louis, Louisville, and Cincinnati, walls crumbled, chimneys toppled, and windows shattered. Five hundred miles away in New Orleans, the earth groaned and trembled. And in Boston, more than 1,100 miles from the epicenter, vibrations from the massive quake set church-bells ringing.

Some people read a spiritual meaning into the frightening event. It was a warning from God, they said, a warning that presaged a greater disaster. Indeed, fifty years later, with the outbreak of the Civil War, the nation would again be torn asunder in a different but no less catastrophic way.

Although no one realized it at the time, another significant event occurred in 1811. In that year, not far from Boston, a child was born, and her destiny was to shake the nation as not even the great earthquake had done. Many years later, she was to write a book that would rouse the conscience of America and the world with its profound indictment of slavery. The book was *Uncle Tom's Cabin,* and its author was Harriet Beecher Stowe.

You have probably read at least one book that has impressed you or influenced you deeply. You may have read a book that altered the way you think, or a book that has even changed your life. But can you imagine a book so powerful as to affect not only the way millions of people think but to change the course of history itself? Such books are rare, but *Uncle Tom's Cabin* was such a book.

Because of its effect on the history of our nation, and because of its enduring influence on people all around the world, *Uncle Tom's Cabin* remains one of the most important books ever written by an American writer.

This writer hopes that after reading *this* book, you will turn to Mrs. Stowe's work and read for yourself the inspiring story that changed the face of America. You may discover, along with critic Edmund Wilson, that *Uncle Tom's Cabin* is a "startling experience . . . a much more remarkable book than one had ever been allowed to suspect." You may also find that, in these days of growing racial tensions, Mrs. Stowe's book will offer you some historical insight and understanding of the forces of prejudice that 130 years after the Civil War, continue to divide and strain our nation.

S.M.C., Covington, Louisiana, 1993

CHAPTER 1

A NEW ENGLAND CHILDHOOD

THE WEATHERED old house that stood on the tree-lined street near the outskirts of Litchfield, Connecticut, presented such a plain face to the world that the casual passerby would hardly have given it a second glance. Had he been invited inside, however, he might have concluded that this was the most extraordinary house in all of New England. Indeed, such was the opinion of many people who visited the house during the early years of the nineteenth century when it was the home of the remarkable Beecher family.

The head of the family was the Reverend Dr. Lyman Beecher, a large man full of vitality and strength. The year 1811 found him presiding over a bustling household that included his wife Roxanna, five children, an aunt, several boarders, two domestic servants, and, outside, a few dogs and cats, a cow, a horse, and assorted chickens and pigs.

Born in 1775, Lyman Beecher was the son of David Beecher, a New Haven blacksmith, and a descendent of Connecticut's first settlers. He was orphaned at an early age and was raised on a farm by an aunt and uncle. By the time he reached young adulthood, he realized that farming would never satisfy his restless mind. Poor but determined, he entered Yale University in 1793 to study theology and was soon converted to the stern Puritanism of Jonathan Edwards. Several years later, armed with a Doctor of Divinity degree, the brilliant young man set out to make his mark on the world.

In 1810, after serving at a church on Long Island, Dr. Beecher was appointed minister of the Congregational Meeting in Litchfield. At the time, politics in Connecticut were still the domain of the church, and Congregationalism was the official religion of the state, so Dr. Beecher's position was enough to give him importance in the community. But it was not long before his prestige and influence extended far beyond Litchfield.

In the pulpit, Lyman Beecher was a fiery evangelist who preached the doctrine of the Second Great Awakening to his congregation. Living according to the rigid rules of Puritanism, he maintained, did not guarantee salvation. In order to be saved, he said, a person had to experience true spiritual conversion. To become a *real* Christian one had to experience a change of person and submit to the will of the Divine Creator. And only through the gift of grace, he warned, could a person be reconciled with God.

Dr. Beecher worked tirelessly to spread his message, and his powerful oratory attracted thousands of people. They flocked to hear his thundering sermons and his passionate denunciations of evils that ranged from dancing to dueling, from Sunday mail delivery to Unitarianism. His sermons condemning alcoholic beverages and drinking became famous throughout New England and inspired a nationwide temperance movement. To his many followers, religion had never seemed so exciting. Eventually, Dr. Beecher's position as leader of the new evangelicalism would make his name famous throughout the country and earn him recognition as the most influential clergyman of his time.

At home, Lyman Beecher dominated his large family with his forceful personality. He drilled moral and religious values into his children and taught them that a life of service to one's fellow people was the noblest of callings. To encourage his children to think for themselves, he trained them to argue and debate about theological issues. While stressing his own interpretations of the divine word, he warned them not to accept ideas simply because they were reputed to be orthodox, but to decide for themselves if these ideas agreed with the Scriptures. In the often heated nightly debates around the kitchen table, he urged them to stretch their minds. Above all, he instilled in his children a deep sense of social responsibility, and an almost compulsive need to excel in all they did.

In the end, his rigorous training bore fruit. The eventual accomplishments of Lyman Beecher's children more than justified his reputation as the father of more brains than any other man in America. Of his thirteen children, eleven grew to adulthood. All seven of his sons became clergymen, and three of his four daughters became famous.

But Lyman Beecher was not always stern. A man of great physical energy, he could also be boisterously playful. Much to the astonishment and amusement of the neighbors, he built a set of parallel bars in the backyard of the Litchfield house and swung on them like a monkey. He kept an enormous pile of sand in the cellar and, when the weather was bad, he worked off energy by shoveling sand from one side of the cellar to the other. He enjoyed roughhousing with his children, and in quieter moments he entertained them with his violin and amused them with wonderful stories.

Lyman Beecher's wife, Roxanna Foote Beecher, was a soft-spoken, well-educated woman whose gentleness and patience contrasted strongly with her husband's energetic nature. Although Lyman Beecher's fame was large, his income was small, so Roxanna had to use both ingenuity and thrift to make sure that the household ran smoothly. The model of a good New England housewife, she cooked, cleaned, washed, and sewed. She took in boarders to help with expenses. She was a gracious hostess to her husband's many guests. And she saw to it that all the Beecher children were well scrubbed and well behaved.

On June 14, 1811, the busy routine of the household

was temporarily interrupted when Roxanna gave birth to a baby girl. She was the seventh child born to Lyman and Roxanna. A noisy throng of young Beechers eagerly welcomed their new sister into the world. Catherine, the eldest, was ten years old. Then, descending in age, came William Edward, Mary, and George.

They peered at the newcomer in the cradle with bright, curious eyes. She was named Harriet Elizabeth, and she reminded them of their other little sister, also named Harriet, who had died in infancy three years earlier. But as the days passed, it became clear that this second tiny Harriet was a survivor. Gradually, the excitement and novelty of a new little Beecher diminished, and the family returned to its normal round of activity.

As little Harriet grew, she adapted quickly to life among the busy Beechers, who now called her by the affectionate name of "Hatty." She was a pretty child, small for her age, with intelligent blue-gray eyes and thick, brown curls that framed her face. Young though she was, Hatty had a wonderful comic sense and often sent the family into gales of laughter with her sparkling conversation and her droll "monkey faces." A sturdy bundle of energy, Hatty threw herself into the thick of things, always willing to help and eager to please. When her father asked the children to help stack the winter's supply of wood or to remove stones from the garden, Harriet always leapt cheerfully to the task, causing her father to remark, "If only Hatty were a boy now, she'd do more 'n any of 'em."[1]

It was not the first time that Lyman Beecher had expressed the desire that his daughter had been a son, nor was it to be the last. "Wisht it had been a boy,"[2] he had remarked with disappointment when she was born. He had planned careers as ministers for all his sons, and he had hoped for another son to dedicate to the important task of saving souls. Several years later, when Hatty was six, he wrote to a friend, "Hatty is a genius . . . I would give a hundred dollars if she were a boy."[3] Although Lyman Beecher loved his daughter and was to remain forever the most important influence on her life, he gave her little of the attention that he lavished on his sons. The most a girl in the nineteenth century could hope to be was a wife and mother.

In 1813, two years after Hatty was born, Lyman Beecher's wish for another son was fulfilled when Roxanna gave birth to a boy who was named Henry Ward. And in 1815, Roxanna delivered yet another son who was given the name Charles.

Hatty doted on her little brothers, especially Henry Ward, who became her favorite playmate and closest companion. The children were inseparable. They played together and, as children do, they got into mischief. One day, Hatty discovered a paper bag full of tulip bulbs that their mother's brother had sent from New York. She persuaded Henry Ward and Charles that they were onions "such as grown people ate." Anxious for a treat, the children devoured the contents of the bag only to be disappointed by the odd, sweetish taste which was not what they expected onions to taste like. When Roxanna looked in on them, the children told her excitedly that they had found a bag of onions and eaten them all.

Years later, Hatty recalled that her mother had shown "not even a momentary expression of impatience," but had said, "My dear children, what you have done makes Mamma very sorry. These were not onions but roots of beautiful flowers, and if you had let them alone we should have next summer in the garden great beautiful red and yellow flowers such as you never saw."[4] Hatty remembered how miserable she had felt as she looked at the empty paper bag.

Then came the day when Roxanna became so ill that she was confined to bed. In the weeks that followed, Hatty was allowed to visit her mother only a few minutes each day. One afternoon, she tiptoed to the bedside and found her mother, propped up among the pillows, smiling gently at her. That night, Hatty dreamed joyfully that her mother had gotten well. But her happiness on awakening was shattered by the news that her mother had passed away. "My dream was indeed a true one," Hatty said later. "She was forever well."[5]

Hatty was just four years old when Roxanna Beecher died of tuberculosis. Too young to really understand what had happened, she and her little brothers were frightened and confused by the tears of the older children, the somber mourning clothes, and the burial service. When the children asked where their mother was, they were told at one time that she had gone to heaven and at another time that she had been buried in the ground. Several days after the funeral, Catherine discovered three-year-old Henry Ward digging furiously in the garden. When Catherine asked what he was doing, he replied with cool logic, "Why, I'm going to heaven to find Mamma."[6]

Lyman Beecher was crushed by Roxanna's death. Without the wife on whom he depended for emotional support, he felt "a sort of terror, like that of a child suddenly shut out alone in the dark."[7] He felt incapable of dealing with day-to-day concerns, so the burden of caring for the family fell on fifteen-year-old Catherine. Strong minded and energetic, Catherine managed to run the household and to serve as substitute mother to her younger brothers and sisters while pursuing her own education. Hatty began to rely heavily on Catherine for support and comfort, a dependency that was to continue for many years. But in the weeks following her mother's death, Hatty was so sad and depressed that her father decided to send her to stay with her mother's relatives for a while.

Grandmother Foote and Aunt Harriet Foote (for whom Hatty had been named) lived in a little white farmhouse in the hamlet of Nut Plains. It was a cozy, cheerful home, and the two old ladies did all they could to make the child feel welcome and loved. For the first time in her life, Hatty found herself the center of attention. She enjoyed being in the limelight, but there were moments when she wished she were back in Litchfield. Used to playing rough-and-tumble games with her brothers, Hatty had grown into a tomboy, but at Nut Plains she was expected to act like a lady and was forbidden to climb trees and fish in Long Island Sound. Aunt Harriet insisted that little girls should move gently, speak softly, and say "yes, ma'am" and "no, ma'am." She taught Hatty how to sew and knit and made sure that she practiced these useful skills daily. Hatty was so bored by these "feminine arts" that, for the rest of her life, she avoided sewing and knitting unless necessity drove her to them.

A staunch, high-church Episcopalian, Aunt Harriet firmly believed in class distinctions. People, she said, should learn "their place" and act according to their station in life. To ensure that her niece knew her own "place," she took Hatty to the Episcopalian church on Sunday mornings, and afterward, at home, instructed her in catechism. Out of respect for Lyman Beecher's beliefs, Aunt Harriet made sure that her young charge learned not only the Episcopal but the Congregational catechism as well.

The household servants, Dinah and Harry, were also present at the catechism lessons in the dining room. They were the first black people Hatty had ever met, and she enjoyed the deference they showed her by calling her "Miss Harriet." It was nice to feel superior, but, at the same time, Hatty felt that something was very wrong. If Dinah and Harry were children of God, as Aunt Harriet said, why were they not treated as equals? Why was their "place" in life so different from hers? It was a question that was to disturb Hatty for many years to come.

The elderly ladies made sure that four-year-old Hatty learned to read during her stay at Nut Plains. Every day, Grandmother Foote read aloud to the child. When she chose selections from the works of Dr. Samuel Johnson, Hatty was bored to tears. But when Grandmother Foote read from the Bible, Hatty was delighted and amused. The old lady seemed to think of the apostles as dear friends, and would comment on their remarks. "There he is again, now; that's just like Peter," she would say of the fisherman. "He's always so ready to put in."[8]

Grandmother Foote was also fond of reading poems, and from her Hatty inherited her lifelong love of poetry. Hatty had a remarkable memory, and, at her grandmother's knee, she began the habit of memorizing scores of poems and hymns, as well as long passages from the Bible, from which she readily quoted later in life.

When, in the summer of 1816, it was time to return home to Litchfield, Hatty said a tearful good-bye to the old ladies. Grandmother Foote and Aunt Harriet Foote had treated the motherless child with kindness and indulgence; they had made her feel special. Forever after, Hatty was to remember her grandmother's house as a "paradise" where everything "spoke of bright hours of love."[9]

That fall, Hatty was enrolled in Madame Kilbourne's school where she became an avid student. Catherine, pleased by her little sister's progress, wrote in a letter, "Hatty is a very good girl . . . she has learned to read fluently . . . and will make a very good scholar."[10]

In 1817, shortly before Hatty's sixth birthday, Lyman Beecher remarried. Their new stepmother, a cool-mannered young woman named Harriet Porter, was so beautiful that at first the children regarded her with awe. But the new Mrs. Beecher was also intelligent and devout, and soon won the admiration, if not the affection, of everyone in the family. A year later, she gave birth to a baby boy who was named Frederick. In the years that followed, she was to bear her husband three more little Beechers, thus raising the number of Lyman Beecher's children to twelve.

Mrs. Beecher tried valiantly to make ends meet on her husband's meager salary of eight hundred dollars per year, but eventually the strain of raising a household full of children under near-poverty circumstances took its toll. As the years passed, her health declined, and the family noticed that "Mamma" hardly smiled anymore.

Most of the time, however, Hatty and the younger children were oblivious to the problems of their elders. Throughout her life, Hatty recalled her childhood years with pleasure. She and her brothers spent many happy, carefree hours tramping through the woods, playing games, going fishing, and visiting their grandmother at Nut Plains.

At home, surrounded by a warm and loving family, Hatty listened eagerly as her father discoursed on the religious controversies of the day. But most of all she loved to hear him tell stories about the Beecher family's past. A natural and powerful speaker, Lyman Beecher invested these tales with drama and excitement. He told about his boyhood on Uncle Lot's farm, about Revolutionary War days when his uncle and father had taken up their muskets to fight the British, about his days at Yale, about his courtship of Roxanna and how he had wrestled to convert her to Calvinism, about his first church on Long Island, about his parents and grandparents. It thrilled Hatty to learn about her family. It made her feel connected to history, and to sense her own place in the continuing saga.

One story, however, disturbed Hatty greatly. It was the story of Aunt Mary, her mother's sister, who had died in Litchfield when Hatty was two years old. When Mary was young, she had fallen in love with a handsome West Indian planter. After their wedding, they sailed off to his island plantation where they were greeted by a crowd of mulatto children. Mary was greatly shocked to learn that her husband was the father of all the children, and that their mothers were his black slaves. Her husband promptly explained that the women were his property, and that he saw nothing wrong in breeding new servants from them much as he would breed cattle. He couldn't understand why his wife was so dismayed. But Mary, overcome with misery and shame, could no longer stand to touch her husband or even look at him. She became so ill that it seemed best for her to return to Litchfield. Safely back in Roxanna and Lyman Beecher's home, Mary took to her bed, where she wasted away, day after day, until she died. It was a strange story, and its dark picture of slavery impressed itself on Hatty's mind, along with a dread of something else, something frightening and fearful, to which she could give no name.

Lyman Beecher always ended Aunt Mary's story with a

strong denunciation of slavery. On Sundays, too, he roared out against the sin of slavery so effectively that his congregation was often reduced to tears. At the time, slavery was still legal in Connecticut, but few people owned slaves, and those who did treated them like ordinary servants. The slavery against which Lyman Beecher railed seemed to have nothing to do with slavery in their quiet New England town. Instead, it seemed to be a dreadful horror that existed somewhere far, far away. Years later, when she herself came face to face with the evils of slavery, Hatty would come to understand the shame and revulsion that had crushed her poor aunt's spirit.

Most of the time, Hatty was a merry bundle of energy, always in the thick of things, eagerly trying to make people laugh and smile, anxiously seeking love and praise. But, as she grew older, she began to retreat periodically from the swirling activity of the household. She would sit quietly, with her large eyes seemingly focused on something far away, unseen by others. "Hatty's owling about again," her family would say, ignoring her until the mood had passed. Only Lyman Beecher was concerned about Hatty's daydreaming, saying that people who retired "into the garden of revery" were trying to avoid "unwelcome truth" and thereby risked damnation. But Hatty's apparent detachment was deceiving; she always knew exactly what was going on around her. It was a habit that she was to continue throughout her life.

Now that Hatty knew how to read, her appetite for books was insatiable. She was always searching the house for something to read. In the attic, she found barrels full of old religious pamphlets with long titles that meant little to a six-year-old child. But one day, burrowing deep under a dusty stack of sermons, Hatty found an old, yellowed copy of *The Arabian Nights.* She took her treasure to a quiet corner and was soon lost in the marvelous tales.

When Lyman Beecher realized that his daughter was capable of reading adult books, he allowed her access to his vast collection. In later years, Hatty described her father's study:

*High above all the noise of the house, this room
had to me the air of a refuge and a sanctuary.
Its walls were set round from floor to ceiling with
the friendly, quiet faces of books, and there
stood my father's great writing-chair. . . . Here I
loved to retreat and niche myself down in a
quiet corner with my favorite books around me. I
had a kind of sheltered feeling as I thus sat and
watched my father writing, turning to his books,
and speaking from time to time to himself in a
loud, earnest whisper. I vaguely felt that he was
about some holy and mysterious work quite beyond my little comprehension, and I was careful
never to disturb him by question or remark.*[11]

The books themselves, Hatty said, filled her with "solemn
awe." Among the volumes of sermons and essays, their
dreary titles stamped on dark bindings, there was little to
interest a child. But one day, Lyman Beecher brought home
Cotton Mather's *Magnalia Christi Americana.* The book, a
collection of exciting tales about witches, Indians, and heroic Puritan fathers, proved to be "a mine of wealth" to
Hatty. "What wonderful stories those!" she wrote in later life.
"Stories . . . about my own country . . . that made me feel the
very ground I trod on to be consecrated by some special
dealing of God's Providence."[12]

Learning about the Declaration of Independence, and
the abuses and injustices that had driven her colonial ances-
tors to revolt against the British, made her "swell with indignation." She later recalled that she was "as ready as any of
them to pledge my life, fortune, and sacred honor for such a
cause. The heroic element was strong in me, having come
down . . . from a long line of Puritan ancestry, and . . . it made
me long to do something, I knew not what: to fight for my
country, or to make some declaration on my own account."[13]
Next, she devoured *Pilgrim's Progress* and the novels of Sir
Walter Scott. Her greatest discovery, however, was the astonishing, electrifying poetry of George Gordon, Lord Byron.

In 1821, when Hatty was ten years old, Byron fever was sweeping the nation. Young ladies wept over his poetry and sighed at his portrait. Young men, trying to emulate Byron's romantic, darkly handsome looks, dressed themselves in flowing, open-collared shirts and let their hair grow into untamed curls. At social gatherings in Litchfield, people spoke of the young English nobleman's genius and whispered at the rumors of his wild excesses. His first book of poetry caused a sensation with its pulsing rhythms and images, and its passionate sadness and cynicism. And thousands of feminine hearts were broken when his marriage to a beautiful young woman was announced. Soon after the wedding, however, Byron did some wild thing that caused his wife to leave him. To forget the tragedy in his life, people said, he threw himself recklessly into the Italian and Greek struggles for freedom.

When Hatty heard the story, she was convinced that, no matter what Lord Byron had done, his wife should have forgiven him. Although she puzzled over the meaning of some of Byron's lines, his poetry seemed so full of noble thoughts that, surely, the man himself had a soul worth wrestling for. Had *she* been Lady Byron, she would have rescued him from his dark demons through the strength of her womanly love. Since she could do nothing to save Byron from himself, she contented herself with memorizing page after page of his verses, unaware that fate would someday bring her face to face with the affairs of the romantic poet and his wife.

Hatty's brother, Frederick, had died of scarlet fever in 1820, at the age of one. It was a common cause of death among children at that time. When Hatty was also stricken with a violent attack of the same dread disease, the family worried that she, too, might not survive. But after several weeks in bed, Hatty finally recovered.

In 1822, when Hatty was eleven, another sister, Isabella, was born. Now Hatty was no longer the youngest girl in the family, and she was expected to help care for the baby after school. She had never enjoyed being "babied" herself, and was secretly happy about this added responsibility. Despite her new chores, she still found time for her beloved books. At that time, Hatty's brother Edward wrote, "Harriet reads everything she can lay her hands on, and sews and knits diligently."[14]

For several years, Hatty had been enrolled in the Litchfield Academy where she led her class in achievement. The headmaster, John Brace, inspired her to write well. "Mr. Brace," she said later, "exceeded all teachers I ever knew in the faculty of teaching composition."[15] As she did with everything that interested her, Hatty approached writing with enthusiasm. So when Mr. Brace announced that each student was required to submit an essay by the end of the term, twelve-year-old Hatty set to work immediately.

When parents and visitors assembled at the Litchfield Academy graduation ceremonies that year, they were treated to a reading of two prize-winning essays. The first prize, Mr. Brace announced, had been awarded by the unanimous vote of the judges to a twenty-five-hundred-word essay entitled, *Can the Immortality of the Soul Be Proved by the Light of Nature?* The essay, a remarkable treatise on the celestial origin and destiny of mankind, was closely reasoned, cogent, and well-written. "Who wrote that composition?" Lyman Beecher asked, when the applause died down. Hatty never forgot how her father's face glowed with pride and delight when he heard Mr. Brace answer: "Your daughter, sir." She later wrote, "It was the proudest moment of my life."[16]

Harriet Elizabeth Beecher had achieved her first public acclaim as an author. Her career as a writer was launched. Honors and accolades would be heaped on her in later years, but none would ever mean as much to her as the look of pleasure on her father's face that night.

CHAPTER 2

SCHOOL AND CHURCH

IF LYMAN BEECHER had been forced to admit which of his many children was closest to his heart, he probably would have conceded that his eldest daughter, Catherine, was his favorite. Intelligent and good-humored, Catherine could always be relied on to do the right thing and to lift everyone's spirits. When Roxanna Beecher died, it was Catherine who ran the household. And it was Catherine to whom her brothers and sisters turned when they needed encouragement and comforting. Ten years older than Hatty, Catherine was, next to Lyman Beecher, the dominant influence on Hatty's early years.

Born in an age in which the highest position to which a woman could aspire was that of wife and mother, Catherine had radical ideas about the role of women. She believed that women should be able to develop their minds and talents, and to have careers of their own, even if they were married and had children. Like all of Lyman Beecher's children, Catherine was not content merely to hold a belief; she felt compelled to put it into action and to convince others to do the same. At a time when few educational opportunities were open to women, Catherine managed to obtain a first-rate education and, at the age of twenty, she became a teacher in New Haven, Connecticut.

When, in the summer of 1821, Catherine was courted by a young Yale professor named Alexander Metcalfe Fisher, all the Beechers were pleased. Every weekend, Professor Fisher traveled to Litchfield. After church services, he and Catherine would play duets on the piano and talk endlessly about a variety of subjects from astronomy to poetry. In September, Catherine resumed her job in New Haven only to return home at New Year's with the announcement that she and Professor Fisher planned to be married after he returned from a trip to Europe. All the Beechers were delighted by the romantic turn of events. Mrs. Beecher was especially happy to have her competent stepdaughter at home. She was soon to give birth to another child, and she needed Catherine's help in running the household.

It was decided that Hatty should be kept out of earshot when the birth occurred, so she was bundled aboard a stagecoach and sent off to visit Grandmother and Aunt Harriet Foote. Hatty was always pleased to spend time with the old ladies, and she was thrilled to discover that Uncle Samuel Foote was at Nut Plains, too. It was a happy vacation for Hatty. Uncle Samuel was a sea captain, home from a voyage, and he entertained Hatty with marvelous tales about pirates, storms, and strange, exotic lands.

Spring was in the air when, on April 1, 1822, Professor Fisher set sail on the *Albion,* bound for Liverpool. He promised that he would write, but poor Catherine was never to hear from her fiancé again. After a few months, rumors about a terrible shipwreck on the coast of Ireland reached Litchfield. Then came the tragic news that the *Albion* was lost, and that Professor Fisher had drowned at sea.

Lyman Beecher tried to comfort Catherine about the state of her beloved's soul. "We can hope," he said, "that in the last terrible moments . . . that the miracle happened, and he knew and accepted the sublime goodness of God."[1] But Catherine was tortured by doubts. She worried that Professor Fisher had not been "saved" and that he might be suffering the torments of hell.

According to John Calvin, upon whose doctrines the

church in New England was based, everything that happened in the world was preordained by God. Mankind was sinful by nature, and God had decided, at the moment of Creation, who would enjoy eternal life in Paradise and who would suffer eternal damnation. Calvin said that neither prayer nor good works could alter whatever God had foreordained; people were prisoners of the destiny that God had ordered for them.

This harsh doctrine had almost caused the breakup of the church in New England in the early 1700s, until Jonathan Edwards, a Puritan theologian, addressed the problem. According to Edwards, a person had to bow to God's will and joyfully accept whatever destiny God had planned for him. If a person humbly accepted God's will, God would let him know if he were one of the "elect." Divine Grace would give the person a sense of rapturous joy, and he would know that salvation was his. Although a person's fate was predestined, Edwards said that in order to attain eternal salvation, it was necessary to *know* that one had been chosen by God to be saved. People were still prisoners of the Divine Order, but this notion allowed many people to feel better about their own destinies.

Catherine continued to worry about the state of Professor Fisher's soul. He had never told Catherine that he was sure of his own salvation. Professor Fisher had been a good man, but being good was no guarantee of safe conduct into Paradise. The thought of Professor Fisher doomed to eternity in hell was abhorrent to Catherine. She could no longer accept the idea of a wrathful God, or love a God who was unmoved by the sorrows of his creatures. If God had sent his own son, Jesus Christ, to die for the salvation of mankind, surely, Catherine reasoned, he must be a God of love. Sometimes, Catherine admitted, she felt that her thoughts were all "pride, rebellion, and sin." But she continued to struggle with the problem and, many years later, published an extraordinary refutation of Jonathan Edwards's ideas. In the meantime, however, Catherine did not allow this crisis to

dampen her determination or her spirit. Until she could resolve her doubts, Catherine decided "to find happiness in
living to do good."[2]

It was in this state of mind that Catherine went to Hartford in 1824 and opened a school for young women, using
part of the legacy that Professor Fisher had left her in his
will, and taking with her the second Beecher daughter, Mary,
as her only teaching staff.

One day, a few weeks after Catherine's departure, Lyman Beecher came home with dreadful news: "Byron is
dead—gone."[3] To Hatty, Byron's death was much more
tragic than Professor Fisher's. She had memorized Byron's
verses and cherished his image in her secret dreams. She did
not think it strange when her father remarked, "I did hope he
would live to do something for Christ. What a harp he would
have swept!", or when, after a thoughtful pause, Lyman
Beecher continued, "Oh, if Byron could only have talked
with me, it might have got him out of his troubles."[4]

Hatty was sure that if Byron had come to visit her father
in his study, his soul might have been saved. In a state of
depression, she wandered off to a nearby hillside where she
lay down among the daisies and, looking up into the blue
sky, thought of that great eternity into which Byron had
entered. It pained her to think that the poet was not in
heaven but in that other, dreadful place. She had listened
with deep interest when Catherine and Lyman Beecher wrestled with the mystery of life after death. Now, she began to
worry about the state of her own soul, but she hesitated to
approach her father with her doubts. Instead, she brought
her questions to her brother Edward, eight years her senior,
who was studying for the ministry. Gentler and more patient
than their father, Edward helped his little sister dispel her
fears.

Except for visits to Nut Plains, Hatty, who was now thirteen
years old, had never been away from home. She had always
gone to school with her younger brothers, Henry Ward and

Charles. But now that Catherine had established a school for teenage girls, it seemed only natural that Hatty should be one of her sister's pupils. The school was a rousing success, and Catherine would soon need a larger staff. She hoped to train Hatty to become a teacher. What a thrilling opportunity it seemed to the young girl! So, with great excitement, Hatty packed her few belongings and traveled by stagecoach the thirty miles to Hartford.

Hatty was astonished by the bustle and activity of Hartford's busy streets, so different from the quiet village of Litchfield. She found Catherine's school located above a harness store in front of which hung a sign picturing two white horses. "I never shall forget the pleasure and surprise these two white horses produced in my mind when I first saw them," Hatty later wrote.[5] She was even more pleased by the living arrangements that had been made for her. Because family funds were limited, Lyman Beecher had worked out an exchange agreement with Isaac D. Bull, a Hartford druggist. Hatty would board with the Bull family, and Mr. Bull's daughter would live with the Beechers while attending school in Litchfield.

Hatty was delighted with the arrangement. The Bull family were kind, gentle people with whom she soon felt comfortable, and their home was "the very soul of neatness and order."[6] Best of all, for the first time in her life, Hatty had a room of her own. It was a pleasantly furnished little room, and she took care of it each day with "awful satisfaction."[7]

It took longer for Hatty to get used to school. Shy and ill at ease, she despaired of ever making friends with any of the chattering, giggling girls. Two of them, however, reached out to her and made her feel welcome. One was Catherine Ledyard Cogswell, the daughter of a prominent Hartford physician. The other was Georgiana May, whose widowed mother presided over a large family. Both girls were destined to become close, lifelong friends of Hatty's.

Catherine Cogswell was the prettiest, most popular girl in school, and Hatty admired her intelligence and social grace. But Catherine Cogswell's time, Hatty complained privately, was "all bespoken by different girls . . . yet she did keep a little place here and there for me."[8]

It was Georgiana May, a plain, quiet girl, who was to become Hatty's dearest friend. After lessons, the two girls often went walking together down Hartford's busy streets or along the tree-lined banks of the Park River. In a growing intimacy, they gossiped about their lessons, the books they had read, and the poetry they loved, and their hopes and dreams for the future. Hatty, who had never before had a friend to whom she could confide her deepest feelings, talked endlessly. One day, she confessed to Georgiana her secret dream of someday becoming a poet.

At school, Hatty worked diligently at philosophy, Italian, and French. To catch up with the other students, she taught herself Latin. In the evenings, after dinner with the Bull family, Hatty retreated to the cozy silence of her room where she poured out her thoughts on paper. She began work on her first piece of fiction, an epic verse drama she entitled *Cleon.* Cleon, the main character, was a Greek lord who lived in the court of the Roman emperor, Nero. Like her beloved Byron, Cleon spent his life in dissipation and idle luxury. But unlike Byron, Cleon, after much searching and doubting, came to accept the teachings of Christianity—in Beecher fashion. Hatty stayed up late every night, writing furiously by candlelight. She was thrilled by the way the words seemed to flow into her mind in a steady stream. "I filled blank book after blank book with this drama. It filled my thoughts sleeping and waking," Hatty recalled years later.[9]

One day, Catherine burst into Hatty's sanctuary and discovered the notebooks, which she quickly confiscated. She sternly lectured Hatty about wasting time writing poetry. If Hatty had time to write rubbish, Catherine said, she obviously didn't have enough practical work to do to keep her busy. Catherine immediately assigned Hatty the task of studying Butler's *Analogy,* a work that would discipline her mind. But that was not all. Catherine insisted that Hatty prepare herself to teach the *Analogy* to her fellow students. So, every day, Hatty instructed a class of girls as old as herself, barely managing to stay one chapter ahead of her students. The pressure was almost too much for the fourteen-year-old girl. Remembering her feelings at the time, Hatty later wrote, "As I walked the pavements I used to wish that they might sink beneath me if only I might find myself in heaven."[10]

Like all the Beechers, Hatty had a mind of her own, and even Catherine's censure could not crush her love of poetry or her determination to write. She discovered that she could get by with six hours of sleep instead of eight. In defiance of Catherine's wishes, Hatty used the extra hours to write secretly, late at night, in the stillness of her room. It was a habit that she continued throughout her life.

At last, summer came. Hatty said an affectionate farewell to her new friends and went home to Litchfield. With the pressures of school temporarily suspended, Hatty's mood improved. She took long, dreamy walks through the lovely New England countryside, enjoying the wildflowers, the sunshine, and the rippling brooks that flowed nearby. On Sundays, she joined her family in the Beecher pew and listened quietly to her father's sermons.

One clear, fresh Sunday morning in the summer of 1824, Hatty plodded off to church, expecting to hear one of Lyman Beecher's usual sermons. "Most of father's sermons were as unintelligible to me as if he had spoken in Choctaw," she later confessed.[11] It was a special Communion Sunday, and Hatty longed to be one of the "elect." She tried to feel sorry for her sins, knowing that repentance was the first step to conversion, but her mind was distracted by the beauty of the day, the singing of the birds, and the scent of warm hay drifting across the meadows. As she looked around at the parishioners entering the church, she thought to herself, "There won't be anything for me today; it is all for these grown-up Christians."[12] Only those who were "under conviction" of their own salvation would be allowed to take communion.

But that Sunday, Lyman Beecher surprised his daughter when he began to preach. Instead of a thunderous lecture about the wrath of God and the sins of man, Lyman Beecher delivered what he called a "frame" sermon, a spontaneous outpouring of deep feeling. Putting aside his usual hairsplitting subtleties, he spoke eloquently about Christ's great love and compassion. He used as his text the words of Jesus recorded in the Gospel of John: "Behold, I call you no longer servants, but friends." When her father roared out passionately, "Come, then, and trust your soul to this faithful friend!" Hatty knew that the message was meant for her. "Oh, how much I needed just such a friend," she thought to herself. Jesus would take her to his heart, sins and all. On the walk home, her "whole soul was illumined with joy."[13]

When Lyman Beecher came back to his study, Hatty threw herself into his arms, saying, "Father, I have given myself to Jesus, and He has taken me." Lyman Beecher looked tenderly at his daughter and, with tears gathering in his eyes, said, "Is it so? Then has a new flower blossomed in the kingdom this day."[14]

Lyman Beecher accepted Hatty's conversion as a fact. But some people regarded it with suspicion. At the time, most people believed that true conversion could happen only after intensive soul-searching. Catherine, still struggling through her own spiritual crisis, was skeptical that Hatty could enter the fold so easily, "without being first chased all over the lot by the shepherd,"[15] and her sharp comments cast a black cloud over Hatty's happiness.

Lyman Beecher's close friend, the pastor of the First Congregational Church in Hartford, added to Hatty's distress. "Harriet, do you feel that if the universe should be destroyed, you could be happy with God alone?" he asked solemnly. Hatty tried to imagine such a state of affairs, and managed to stammer out, "Yes, sir." Eyeing her gravely, he continued: "You realize, I trust, in some measure at least, the deceitfulness of your heart, and that in punishment for your sins God might justly leave you to make yourself as miserable as you have made yourself sinful?" Again, Hatty whispered, "Yes, sir."[16] The pastor smiled and dismissed her. But Hatty began to worry that her "heavenly friend" might abandon her, and wondered if she would ever again experience the joyous ecstasy she had felt on the Sunday of her conversion.

When Hatty returned to school in September 1825, she was happy to be reunited with her friends, Georgiana May and Catherine Cogswell, but her pleasure was short-lived. Had she been allowed to live the life of an ordinary schoolgirl, Hatty might have conquered her religious doubts quickly and recovered her sunny outlook on life. But Catherine Beecher had other plans for her fourteen-year-old sister. Catherine decided that Hatty was ready to take on additional teaching responsibilities.

Every morning, Hatty was up before sunrise. All day long, she attended classes in which she was either teacher or student. In the evenings, she studied Latin and mathematics (which she hated), and prepared the lessons that she would teach the next day. This grueling schedule left her with little time to indulge in the ordinary dreams and pastimes of an adolescent girl. She worried constantly about her schoolwork, about her teaching, and about the state of her soul. She poured out her heart in letters to Edward, her kind, handsome brother. "My whole life is one continued struggle: I do nothing right. . . . I am beset behind and before, and my sins take away all my happiness. But that which most constantly besets me is pride—I can trace almost all my sins back to it."[17]

In March 1826, Lyman Beecher announced that he had accepted an offer to be the pastor of the Hanover Street Church in Boston. Although he was a famous preacher, his salary in Litchfield was still only eight hundred dollars a year—not nearly enough to feed and clothe his growing family. (A son, Thomas, had been born in 1824, and another son,

James, would be added to the family in 1828.) The new position in Boston would pay two thousand dollars a year. Although the move made financial sense for the family, Hatty was upset. She was still brooding about her religious problems, and her depression was compounded by a feeling of insecurity brought on by the breakup of the Litchfield home.

She was grateful, therefore, when Lyman Beecher withdrew her from Catherine's school, brought her to the new home in Boston, and enrolled her in a day school. Hatty hoped that her father would be able to help her out of her misery, but Lyman Beecher had little time for his daughter. Away from Catherine and her friends in Hartford, her spiritual torment grew worse. She moped around the house and had trouble sleeping at night. When Mrs. Beecher reprimanded her moody stepdaughter, Hatty would burst out in shrill, nervous laughter. Only Edward, now a minister in a Boston church, seemed to understand. He listened patiently to Hatty and tried to help her reconcile the contradictions she perceived between a God of wrath and her soul-friend, Jesus.

Back in Hartford, Catherine's school, now called the Hartford Female Seminary, was bursting at the seams. In 1827, Catherine ordered the construction of a new building to accommodate the increasing numbers of students and teachers. She was very busy, but she was never too busy to care about Hatty. One day, she received a disturbing letter in which Hatty had written, "I don't know as I am fit for anything, and I have thought that I could wish to die young, and let the remembrance of me and my faults perish in the grave, rather than live, as I fear I do, a trouble to every one. How perfectly wretched I often feel—so useless, so weak, so destitute of all energy."[18]

Clearly worried, Catherine wrote to Edward, suggesting that Hatty return to Hartford. "If she could come here, it might be the best thing for her, for she can talk freely to me. I can get her books, and Catherine Cogswell, Georgiana May, and her friends here could do more for her than anyone in

Boston, for they love her, and she loves them very much."[19]
Catherine wrote to Lyman Beecher, too, offering other rea-
sons for sending Hatty back to Hartford: "I can do better in
preparing her to teach . . . for I know best what is needed."[20]

Hatty wasn't the only nineteenth-century teenager to
drive herself and her family crazy. All over the country, sensitive adolescents raised in the stern Puritanical tradition
were undergoing similar agonies. Girls who were unable to
overcome their "natural depravity" found release in fits of
fainting and hysteria. Boys sometimes gave up hope and ran
away, abandoning themselves to lives at sea or wild abandon
in cities. Those who managed to work through their confusion often turned into adults with rock-solid, narrow con-
victions.

Back under Catherine's protective eye, Hatty began to
feel better. When summer came, she once again visited
Grandmother Foote and Aunt Harriet. But her dark thoughts
continued. Not even the presence of Uncle Samuel Foote
could alter her moodiness. Uncle Samuel, recently retired
from the sea, talked about a trip to the American West from
which he and his new wife had just returned. Engrossed in
her own thoughts, Hatty paid little attention to his enthusi-
astic descriptions of the regions that lay beyond the Appalachians. She barely noticed when he raved about the town
of Cincinnati, a "beautiful spot, right on the river, and growing by leaps and bounds!"[21]

When Hatty returned to Hartford in the fall of 1827, she
found her older sisters in a state of excitement. Catherine's
new school building was nearing completion, and Mary was
planning her wedding to a young attorney. Now sixteen,
Hatty was at an age when most girls had romantic thoughts.
But she showed little interest in her sister's romance, or
romance of any kind. When she was introduced to boys her
age, she would retreat shyly or discourage conversation with
a sharp remark. The only men she cared about were her
brothers. "I love to hear sisters speak well of their brothers,"
she wrote. "There is no pride I can so readily tolerate as
pride of relationship."[22]

The impressive new school building opened with more than a hundred pupils. When classes resumed, Hatty was once again buried under a heavy schedule of teaching and studying. In addition to her other teaching duties, she now taught a class in rhetoric. She took drawing lessons and learned to paint in oils and watercolors, but she had little time to develop her artistic talent.

Hatty did manage, however, to keep up a lengthy correspondence with Edward, speculating in depth about the nature of God's love for mankind. Edward faithfully responded to all her letters and, because of him, she once again took up her old habit of reading every book in sight, trying to recapture her dream of someday becoming a great writer. She began to study seriously the business of writing, and in a letter to Mary Dutton, a fellow teacher, she said that she had been writing "in imitation of Dr. Johnson's style— think it is improving me by giving me a command of language."[23] By the age of eighteen, Hatty had planted her feet firmly on the path that would someday lead her to worldwide fame.

For the next few years, Hatty followed the same teaching routine. She spent vacations at home in Boston, with the Footes at Nut Plains, and with her brothers who now had churches of their own throughout New England. And she managed, finally, to come to terms with her spiritual problems. In 1830, she wrote to Edward, "I do hope that my long, long course of wandering and darkness and unhappiness is over, and that I have found in Him who died for me all, and more than all, I could desire."[24]

By now, writing had become a compulsive habit with Hatty, and she indulged her habit by writing long letters to her family and friends. Her letters showed no interest in the politics or issues of the day, but dealt mainly with religion and her own feelings. But they showed that Hatty had changed for the better. Describing her new approach to life in a letter to Georgiana May, Hatty wrote, "I have come to a firm resolution to count no hours but unclouded ones, and to let all others slip out of my memory and reckoning as quickly as possible. . . . I am trying to cultivate a general spirit of kindliness towards everybody. Instead of shrinking into a corner to notice how other people behave, I am holding out my hand to the right and to the left. . . . In this way I find society full of interest and pleasure."[25]

Throughout Hatty's troubled adolescence, Lyman Beecher was so involved in his own concerns that he was hardly aware of his daughter's problems. While Hatty was battling her private demons, Lyman Beecher was busy waging political war against the Unitarians and campaigning for a hundred causes, including, among others, the abolition of Sunday steamboat excursions, lotteries, and the consumption of liquor. He rallied the young men in his congregation to join in the fray, and these zealous crusaders, constantly seeking Lyman Beecher's advice, were forever knocking at the front door. Although she admitted them politely, Hatty paid little attention to the young men. She hardly noticed the brilliant young scholar with the mischievous eyes named Calvin Stowe who was one of her father's most frequent visitors. Nor did he give any reason to suppose that he had noticed her, either.

By 1832, when she was twenty-one years old, Hatty was a full-time teacher at Catherine's school. She thought of herself as plain and unattractive, but to others she appeared a lovely young woman, with a small, graceful figure. Her oval face, with its high forehead, large eyes, finely shaped straight nose, and gentle mouth, was framed by rich, dark hair. Hatty imagined that she would never marry, and that, for the next few years at least, she would continue teaching at Catherine's school. But an extraordinary event was to propel her— and all the Beechers—into a future that none of them anticipated.

It began when Lyman Beecher caused a sensation in Boston by delivering a series of stirring sermons on temperance. What his congregation didn't know was that while they listened to Dr. Beecher thunder against the evils of drink, the cellar of the church was stacked high with barrels of rum belonging to a liquor merchant to whom Lyman Beecher had rented the space for use as a warehouse. One day the church caught fire. By the time the fire fighters arrived, the situation was out of control. The barrels of rum had burst into bright blue flames, and the smell of liquor filled the air. Then, one by one, the barrels exploded, shaking the building and filling the air with hundreds of temperance pamphlets that had been stored in an upper room. The pamphlets drifted slowly through the sky over the neighborhood, falling gently here and there. While the fire raged out of control, a crowd gathered, and as the church burned to the ground, the firemen laughed and people sang and joked about "Beecher's broken jug."

It was a disaster, and very embarrassing. But Lyman Beecher, who never lost his sense of humor, took it in stride. "Well, my jug's broke, all right," he said, cheerfully.[26] It was time to make new plans.

CHAPTER 3

CINCINNATI

NEVER ONE to cry over spilt milk, Lyman Beecher immediately laid plans for a new church. Soon after the plans were set in motion, he received an astonishing offer from the trustees of the Lane Theological Seminary, a new school that was being built in the far-off western city of Cincinnati, Ohio. The trustees had decided that only one man could fulfill their dream of turning the school into the "Yale of the West." That man was Lyman Beecher. They offered him the presidency of the school, plus an operating budget of seventy thousand dollars. It was an offer Lyman Beecher couldn't afford to refuse. Before accepting, however, he wanted to meet with the trustees and inspect the building—and Cincinnati—for himself. Together with Catherine, who immediately began dreaming of opening a college for women next to the seminary, Lyman Beecher set out for the West.

Hatty was left behind in Hartford to continue her daily round of teaching, reading, and endless letter writing. The days dragged on. She felt tired and listless all the time. She seemed to be stuck in a rut where everything was tedious and pointless. She yearned for something—she didn't know what—to enter her life. Only love, or the idea of love, sustained her. "The desire to love forms, I fear, the great motive for all my actions . . . " she wrote to Edward at the time.[1] Hatty may have craved earthly love—she was, after all, an attractive young woman—but it was only divine love about which she talked in her letters, expressing almost all her feelings in religious terms. "There is a Heaven," she wrote, "a world of love, and love after all is the life blood, the existence, the all in all of mind."[2] Someday, Hatty would look back on these days as the end of a period in which her "mind lived only in emotions" and all her real "history was internal."[3]

But real history was about to change Hatty's life. Dr. Beecher and Catherine returned from Cincinnati, filled with enthusiasm and excitement. "The moral destiny of our nation, and all our institutions and hopes . . . turns on the character of the West," Lyman Beecher told his family.[4] The "majestic West" could be saved for Calvinism through the thrilling power of revivals, he declared. An empire might be won for God!

Beyond that, Catherine and Lyman Beecher reported that the campus of Lane Theological Seminary was more beautiful than they had imagined. The buildings were splendid, and there was space for Catherine's school. They were also full of praise for Cincinnati, calling it a "paradise" and a "beehive of Christianity." They raved on and on about the landscape, the climate, the Ohio River, and the cultivated people they had met. Uncle Samuel Foote and his wife, who already lived in Cincinnati, loved it, too. And so on and on and on.

Hatty was not sure how she felt about the whole business. But, then, nobody had asked her opinion. The decision had been made. As soon as the new church in Boston was built and dedicated, most of the Beechers would move to Cincinnati, the Athens of the West. William, recently married, would stay behind, as would Mary and her husband. Henry Ward and Charlie, Hatty's younger brothers, would also remain to continue their schooling. Hatty would be sorry to leave them, but she was pleased by the news that

Edward had accepted an offer to be the president of a new college in Jacksonville, Illinois. Another Beecher would join the westward migration!

The family flew into action. Lyman Beecher dedicated the new church in Boston and was given a fond farewell by his congregation. Catherine made arrangements for the continuation of her school in Hartford. The household was taken apart and the family's possessions were packed in trunks and crates and boxes. The house was filled with nervous excitement. Yet, although confusion reigned around her, Hatty felt suspended in time. Not until she said good-bye to her old home, to her relatives at Nut Plains, and to her friend, Georgiana, did Hatty join in her family's infectious spirit of anticipation.

At last the trip began when, in October 1832, nine members of the Beecher family, with their boxes, crates, and trunks, piled into a stagecoach and set off on the initial leg of their journey. Their first stop was New York City, where Lyman Beecher convinced the trustees of Lane Seminary to add a professor of Biblical literature to the faculty. Describing her father's activities in a letter, Hatty wrote, "the incumbent is to be C. Stowe,"[5] without hinting that she might remember, in any way, the short, stocky young man who used to call on her father.

From New York, the Beechers traveled by steamship to Philadelphia where they once again piled their belongings into a stagecoach. Now, they were truly traveling west! Filled with a heady sense of adventure, their spirits rose even higher. They passed through Pennsylvania, singing hymns and laughing while tossing religious tracts out of the coach to startled people along the way, or, as Hatty reported cheerfully, "peppering the landscape with moral influence."[6]

Beyond Harrisburg, their progress was slowed by the steep roads winding through the wild beauty of the Appalachians, the first mountains that Hatty had ever seen. They crossed the Ohio River at Wheeling (now in West Virginia), and followed its course along bumpy, muddy roads that jolted and flung them and their luggage from one side of the coach to the other. Bruised, shaken up, and splashed with mud, but still in fine humor, the Beechers finally reached Cincinnati on November 14, 1832, five weeks after leaving Boston.

Cincinnati, with a population of nearly thirty thousand, was a booming river port spread over a group of hills on the north bank of the Ohio River. Here were the impressive homes, stately public buildings, and fine schools and churches that Catherine had described. Here, too, was a thriving cultural life, with theaters, lively musical groups, and several literary societies. The seminary and the Beechers's new house were located at Walnut Hills, a picturesque, tree-covered site on the heights above the city.

Cincinnati was much bigger and more interesting than Hatty had imagined. Her first impression was like that of the novelist Charles Dickens, who wrote, "I have not often seen a place that commends itself so favorably to the stranger at first glance."[7] But a closer look was to alter her opinion.

In the 1830s, Cincinnati was a center for the meat-packing industry. Farmers brought their pigs to the city where they were soon slaughtered and transformed into ham and bacon and salt pork that would be shipped east and south. Until they met their demise, the pigs were allowed to roam freely through the city where they grew fat by eating garbage thrown out on the streets by city dwellers. This practice, and the revolting smells that rose from the slaughterhouses near the river, earned the city the nickname of "Porkopolis." Hatty found the whole business "very disgusting," and she was appalled when one day her four-year-old brother, James, actually climbed on the back of a hog and "rode some distance."[8]

Hatty would soon discover that something infinitely more revolting than the pork industry flourished just across the Ohio River in Kentucky, and throughout the South—the vile institution of slavery.

Many years before the Beechers moved to Cincinnati,

slavery in the northern states had been abolished by the generation that had fought in the American Revolution. These same patriots believed that slavery in the South would eventually die as well. They were sure that, besides being immoral and un-Christian, slavery would prove to be too expensive and unprofitable for plantation owners who grew such crops as tobacco and indigo.

Had things gone on as they were, slavery might well have been abandoned. But two inventions—the cotton gin in America and the mechnical spindle in England—changed the course of history. The cotton gin (invented in 1793) did away with the time-consuming method of cleaning cotton by hand, and the mechanical spindle quickly transformed the cotton into fine thread, thus disposing of the obstacles that had stood in the way of producing cotton fabric quickly and economically.

Suddenly, the cotton boom was on, and slavery was no longer a dying institution. Southern planters switched to cotton as their main crop and relied on increasing numbers of slaves to work the vast plantations that spread rapidly across the South. In the northern states and in England, factories sprang up to meet the growing demand for cotton goods. In the South, slaves toiled "from sunup to sundown" under the blazing sun that beat down on the cotton fields, while in the factories, ill-paid workers labored through fourteen-hour days to transform the raw cotton into cloth. The Industrial Revolution was under way, and in the American South, slavery was indispensable.

At the same time, the United States was growing by leaps and bounds. As the thriving young country expanded its western boundaries, opponents of slavery grew increasingly concerned about the spread of the evil institution. In the Missouri Compromise of 1820, Congress extended the Mason-Dixon line to include the 36th parallel as the dividing line between free territories to the north and slave territories to the south. The line not only divided the country between slave and free, it became a symbol of political, social, and economic divisions as well.

When Hatty arrived there in 1832, Cincinnati, located on the dividing line, was a main stop on the Underground Railroad, an escape route used by many slaves who were fleeing north to gain their freedom. Almost everyone who lived in Cincinnati had a strong opinion about slavery. Abolitionists, with a close-up view of the system, spoke out vehemently against it. But Cincinnati's success relied heavily on trade with the South, so it was not surprising that slavery had outspoken supporters among the city's merchants, cotton and tobacco brokers, and riverboat owners. The topic of slavery was on everyone's lips and formed the subject of many heated arguments and debates.

As the weeks and months rolled by, Hatty would form her own opinions on what was to become the greatest moral, economic, and political issue of the times. In the meantime, however, the Beechers were busy getting settled in their new home.

Within a few days after her arrival, Hatty felt homesick for New England, a feeling that would never leave her throughout her long "exile" in Cincinnati. But she had little time to waste in moping; there was too much to be done. She helped her stepmother with household tasks and with the endless sewing and mending a large family required. She helped Catherine make arrangements for the new school in which she herself was to be one of the teachers. Catherine also assigned a special task to Hatty, one that the younger woman found interesting and even a little exciting.

A new geography book for young children was needed, Catherine said, and Hatty was to be its author. It was her first real writing project since Catherine had so abruptly stopped her from writing *Cleon.* Hatty enjoyed assembling the dull facts of geography into a pleasing and interesting narrative. When the manuscript was finished, Catherine delivered it to a Cincinnati publisher. The book was accepted for publication, and Hatty received $187 for her work—more than she had ever earned from teaching.

Several months later, in March 1833, the following advertisement appeared in a newspaper:

A NEW GEOGRAPHY FOR CHILDREN
Carey & Fairbank have in the press, and will
publish in a few days, a Geography for Children
with numerous maps and engravings, upon an
improved plan.
by Catherine E. Beecher [9]

Hatty was shocked to see her sister's name given as the author. The publisher had decided to use Catherine's name because of her reputation as a "brilliant young educator." Although she swallowed the injustice with little comment, Hatty was deeply hurt. A few months later, her feelings were soothed somewhat when a visiting bishop acknowledged Hatty's authorship and praised her "poor little geography,"[10] but she couldn't help feeling betrayed by the way Catherine had taken credit for *her* work.

Catherine's new school, the Western Female Seminary, opened its doors in May 1833. Hatty was pleased that her old friend, Mary Dutton, had agreed to join the teaching staff. But, once again, the drudgery of teaching began to weigh on Hatty's spirits, and she grew increasingly discontent with her life.

She began reading a biography of Madame de Staël, the brilliant French writer who put some of her extravagant, passionate ideas into practice by taking one lover after another. Hatty felt a strong intellectual and emotional kinship with de Staël while recognizing the sharp contrast between the French woman's exciting life and her own dull existence. She wrote to Georgiana May, "in America feelings vehement and absorbing like hers (Madame de Staël's) . . . are repressed, and they burn inward till they burn the very soul. . . . It seems to me the intensity with which my mind has thought and felt on every subject presented to it . . . has withered and exhausted it. . . . Half of my time I am glad to remain in a listless vacancy, to busy myself with trifles, since thought is pain, and emotion is pain."[11]

Unlike the French writer, Hatty had no outlet for the

feelings and emotions that were burning inside her. She had not yet focused on the issue that was dividing the world just outside her door, the issue upon which she would someday focus and direct her passions in a brilliant rush of words that would bring her inner peace while setting the world ablaze.

But Hatty, now twenty-two years old, was, in fact, busying herself with more than "trifles." Her days were filled with activity. She rose at six every morning, arrived at the school at seven, and, after a full day of teaching, continued to work late into the night. She was depressed and tired all the time, and began to write with regularity in an effort to conquer her "mental listlessness."

When the *Western Monthly,* a new magazine, announced a short-story competition, Hatty decided to enter it. Her story, entitled "Uncle Lot," won first prize, and she was awarded fifty dollars. Hatty was elated. Here was proof of her talent. Her wish to be a writer was no longer an idle dream. This small success bolstered her confidence and gave her new insight into her abilities. She made up her mind to devote all her spare time to writing.

Hatty decided to join the Semi-Colon Club, one of Cincinnati's many literary societies. The club, a congenial group of people, included some authors, editors, and even some of her family among its members. Catherine and Uncle Samuel Foote belonged to the Semi-Colon Club. So did James Hall (who was the editor of the *Western Monthly*), Salmon P. Chase (who later became Chief Justice of the Supreme Court), Professor Calvin Stowe, and the professor's new bride, Eliza Tyler Stowe.

At their meetings, Semi-Colon Club members read their compositions aloud to one another. At first, Hatty was timid about reading her writings aloud to the group, but their reception of her initial efforts was so encouraging and friendly that she was soon writing one piece after another to present for the group's entertainment. She submitted some of her pieces for publication and was thrilled when she sold her first piece for fifty dollars. At the time, Hatty was earning five hundred dollars for a full year of teaching. The article had taken only a few hours to write, but in that time she had earned what seemed to her a large sum of money. She loved to write, but the idea that she might someday earn a living with her pen made writing appear even more attractive. Clearly, writing could be a profitable business. From then on, Hatty considered herself to be a professional writer.

Up to this time, Hatty's only social contacts in Cincinnati had been with her family and with the students and faculty at Lane. Now, at the meetings of the Semi-Colon Club, she made new friends. Calvin and Eliza Stowe, especially, treated her with great warmth. Calvin Stowe was a brilliant, young theologian and Hatty was somewhat awestruck in his presence. But she felt comfortable with Eliza Stowe, a delicate, pretty woman with a fine intellect and a gentle personality. Hatty immediately recognized a soul mate in Eliza Stowe, and "fell in love with her directly."[12] Almost instantly, Hatty and Eliza became close friends. They shared the same views and opinions on many topics, attended church together, and talked with one another about events at Lane.

Hatty would have liked to spend more time with Eliza, but that year, 1833, was an eventful time in the Beecher household and everyone seemed to need Hatty's help. Her older brother, William, arrived in Cincinnati. Now a minister, William sought Hatty's advice before talking to Lyman Beecher about criticisms that had been aimed at him by his congregation.

At the dinner table, her brother Charles argued violently with Lyman Beecher against the teachings of Jonathan Edwards. Hatty had to step into the shouting match when Charles announced that he was giving up the ministry. Although, at the time, Hatty's peacemaking efforts failed, Charles eventually did become a minister. But in the meantime, he went to work as a clerk in New Orleans, returning later to Cincinnati with tales of Louisiana plantation life that Hatty would someday use in her famous book.

Hatty was also called on to tend Mrs. Beecher, who was ill and frequently bedridden. Henry Ward was the only Beecher with courage enough to declare that their stepmother was a "cold woman" who was difficult to love. Although Hatty privately agreed with her brother, she waited on her stepmother without complaint.

George, one year older than Hatty, suffered a spiritual crisis that year, and Edward arrived for a visit just in time to help Hatty convince George to continue his divinity studies at Lane.

Henry Ward also arrived in Cincinnati, having just graduated from school in the East. Someday he would be known as the "greatest oratorical advocate of Christ since Paul,"[13] but for now, Henry Ward, who had never taken schoolwork seriously, surprised the family with his new sense of dedication.

Hatty was delighted that Henry Ward was once again with the family. They had been close as children, but had not seen much of one another in recent years. Henry Ward was the only person in the family with whom Hatty felt completely relaxed, the only one to whom she could confide her deepest, most personal thoughts. They shared a wild sense of humor, a trait most of the other Beechers lacked, and it did not take long for Hatty and Henry Ward to regain their old intimacy. Before long, they were laughing uproariously at their private jokes, sending the other Beechers into fits of consternation.

Despite all the family upheavals and all the work, 1833 was a good year for Hatty. She had launched her career as a professional writer; she had gained a new friend in Eliza Stowe; and she was reunited with her beloved brother, Henry Ward Beecher. Hatty looked happily toward the future, wondering what new challenges and surprises life might hold in store.

CHAPTER 4

WITNESS TO SLAVERY

IN 1833, the Beechers were busy with their own concerns, but they were not too busy to notice that slavery was a much uglier problem than any of them had imagined back in New England. Cincinnati, critically located on the borderline between North and South, was the scene of constant disturbances caused by the situation across the Ohio River. Every day, the Beechers were confronted with new evidence that slavery was a harsh and brutal system.

Advertisements for runaway slaves were posted on buildings around the city and appeared almost daily in the Cincinnati newspapers:

> *$100 REWARD will be paid by the undersigned for the apprehension and delivery of ELLEN, a slave, of yellow color, aged about twenty years, high cheek bones; hesitates in her speech; had on when she left a sun bonnet and a dark green worsted dress . . .*
>
> *$50 REWARD for the delivery of JACK, a slave, aged twenty-eight years, black skin, scars on face and neck, mean tempered, about six feet in height; carried with him articles belonging to the undersigned, viz., a silver pocket knife, an iron pot, a peck of corn. . . .* [1]

A few citizens, sickened by the daily spectacle of human misery, had become outspoken abolitionists. But many people were willing to collect rewards for returning fugitives to their owners. Homes suspected of harboring fugitive slaves were raided. Free blacks were captured, put in chains, and transported south. Sad groups of slaves destined for southern auction blocks could be seen on the decks of steamboats on the wharves.

At first, Hatty could scarcely believe what was happening all around her. She read the advertisements for runaway slaves. She read the editorials defending slavery that appeared in the Cincinnati *Journal,* and she tried to understand the reasoning of those who upheld the system. But when she saw captured slaves being led through the streets, she knew that there was nothing that could justify the hopelessness and pain she saw in their eyes. Slavery was dreadful and cruel. She knew it must be stopped. But what could she do about it? Hatty didn't know. She was a small, shy woman, only twenty-two years old. All she could do was look away. But turning away did no good; there was no way to ignore the misery around her.

During the summer of 1833, Hatty was given a closer view of slavery when she was invited to accompany Mary Dutton, her friend and fellow teacher, on a visit to the home of a student who lived across the Ohio River in Kentucky. Since coming to teach at the Western Female Seminary, Mary Dutton had been too busy to spend much time with Hatty. So Hatty looked forward to the trip as an opportunity to spend some leisurely hours with her friend. She did not realize that the brief vacation would someday serve a larger purpose in her life.

After traveling fifty miles down the river by steamboat, and then riding by stagecoach another few miles, Hatty and Mary arrived in the little village of Washington, Kentucky. Their hosts were charming, easygoing people who entertained them graciously. No one in the family seemed to work, except the slaves who handled all the domestic chores in the comfortably arranged house. Everything was different from the sort of life the two young women had known back in New England, where both Hatty and Mary had lived in genteel poverty while practicing the common virtues of work, neatness, and thrift.

One day, Hatty and Mary accompanied their hosts on a visit to a nearby plantation. As they rode up, they were impressed by the sight of the stately plantation house with its row of tall white columns set amid vast rolling fields of tobacco and corn. A velvet lawn surrounded the house, and inside, Hatty was awestruck by the elegantly furnished, spacious rooms. Later that day, Hatty would see the small slave cabins clustered out of sight behind the house where she silently noted the sharp contrast between the master's mansion and the humble dwellings of his slaves.

The owner of the plantation greeted his visitors jovially. He was a good-natured man, and prior to her visit, Hatty had been pleased to hear that he had a reputation for being kind to his slaves. He took Hatty and Mary on a tour of the estate. They saw slaves engaged in various kinds of work, and the slaves seemed to be contented; but Hatty found it difficult to accept the fact that slaves had no ordinary human rights. They could be well treated, as these slaves were or seemed to be, or they could be grossly mistreated. Husbands and wives could be separated from one another at any moment; their families could be destroyed; children could be torn from their mothers' arms, never to see one another again. They were property that could be bought and sold at the master's whim and, like most slaves, they could expect to be sold at least once in their lives. Still, Hatty had decided that the slaves on this plantation were fortunate to have a kind master—until an incident that evening caused her to think otherwise.

After a lavish dinner that Hatty thought sinfully extravagant, the master commanded some of the slaves to perform for the guests. One little black boy caught Hatty's attention with his bright eyes and appealing smile. The master ordered the child to perform one acrobatic stunt after another and, as the child capered about, the man made rude comments and laughed condescendingly. It was plain to Hatty that the man had no more concern for the child than he had for the hunting dogs that she had seen follow faithfully at his heels.

Mary, wondering if Hatty shared her disgust, glanced over at her friend, but Hatty's expression told her nothing. Hatty was "owling about" again and seemed oblivious to everything around her. In fact, Hatty was outraged by the man's behavior, but she controlled her expression and said nothing.

A few days later, their hosts took Hatty and Mary to church. During the service, Hatty noticed a beautiful young woman seated in a nearby pew. The woman, with her pale golden skin, dark soulful eyes, and soft black hair, had a kind of exotic beauty that puzzled Hatty. When she questioned her hosts about the woman, Hatty was told that the woman was a quadroon and that she was a slave belonging to Mr. So and So.

What did that mean? With growing horror, Hatty realized that the beautiful young woman, who was one-quarter black and three-quarters white, was born of an unholy union between a white master and a mulatto slave woman. She tried not to think of the terrors life must hold for this poor, helpless woman who had no means of resisting her master's desires. The quadroon had no way to protect herself; she had no rights at all. She was the property of a man who could inflict his will on her whenever he chose and, when he no longer had any use for her, he could sell her to the highest bidder.

Hatty remembered again the story that her father had told her as a child, the story about how her Aunt Mary Foote had married a slaveholder and the despair to which her aunt had been driven after seeing her husband's mulatto slave children. Hatty knew that it was not uncommon for a slaveholder to have both a wife and slave mistresses, and to have children with all of them. She wondered what kind of moral somersaults men used to condone such behavior. How could they so dishonor their wives and themselves in this way? How could they abandon their illegitimate children, their own flesh and blood, to lives in bondage? Surely, no civilized Christian man would so outrageously debase the laws of decency this way. But now, with her own eyes, Hatty had seen a woman who was condemned, by her own white father, to a life of slavery.

Once again, the unsettled feelings that had troubled Hatty in adolescence surged up inside her. She tried to drive the disturbing image of the quadroon slave from her thoughts, but like the scene of the master treating the little black boy like a trained monkey, the picture of the sad, lovely woman was branded on her mind. A day would come when Hatty would reach into her memory for these images and thoughts, and they would come to life on the pages of a book that was destined to change the world. But at the time, Hatty gave no outward clue to the thoughts and feelings that were growing to maturity inside her.

> Years later, Mary Dutton said of the visit to Kentucky, "Harriet did not seem to notice anything in particular that happened, but sat much of the time as though abstracted in thought. When the negroes did funny things and cut up capers, she did not seem to pay the slightest attention to them. Afterwards, however, in reading Uncle Tom, I recognized scene after scene of that visit portrayed with the most minute fidelity, and knew at once where the material for that portion of the story had been gathered."[2]

Hatty was happy to return home to her family, to her new friend Eliza Stowe, and to the free soil of Cincinnati. She threw herself into work, writing stories drawn from her memories of New England. The words flew from her pen, filling the pages with wonderful Yankee characters who spoke with the wry humor and salty wisdom of her native home. Several months later, a few of her stories and character sketches were published. As each piece appeared in print, signed "by Miss Harriet E. Beecher," Hatty's resolve to one day make a living as a writer increased.

When school opened in the fall of 1833, Hatty resumed her daily round of teaching and household chores. She was in a happier, more energetic mood than she had been for a long time. In her spare time, she worked on her writing, visited with Eliza Stowe, and, with Eliza and Calvin Stowe, attended meetings of the Semi-Colon Club where she read her stories to a growing number of admirers.

Nearly everyone in the Beecher family was in splendid spirits that fall, especially Lyman Beecher. Lane Theological Seminary was an outstanding success; his plans for training ministers to convert the West to Calvinism were becoming a reality. The seminary opened its doors to welcome nearly a hundred students for the fall semester, and for a while at least, Lyman Beecher didn't seem to mind that many of the new students, led by a radical young man named Theodore Weld, were active abolitionists.

Beecher was strongly opposed to slavery but, unlike the abolitionists, he favored gradual reform. From the pulpit, he denounced the institution of slavery, calling it a sin and a moral evil, but he thought that the abolitionists were wrongheaded, and he refused to side with them. He believed that calling for an immediate end to slavery would only provoke violence, cause the South to stiffen its resistance, and prolong the problem. Immediate emancipation would wreak havoc on the economy of the South, and it would thrust the blacks into a world for which they were not prepared. Before they were freed, the blacks needed to become Christians and they needed to be educated so that they would be able to take care of themselves. The problem would eventually be solved, Lyman Beecher said, when southerners awoke to their moral duty, freed their slaves, and arranged for them to be transported to a colony in Africa.

Back in Boston, Lyman Beecher had argued these points in a vehement public debate with William Lloyd Garrison, the founder of the abolitionist movement. But now, in the fall of 1833, he sensed no threat from Theodore Weld or the clique of abolitionists at Lane.

What Lyman Beecher didn't realize was that the seminary's chief benefactor, Arthur Tappan, was an ardent abolitionist, and that Tappan had encouraged Theodore Weld to set up a core of agitators at Lane. A few months later, Weld wrote a letter to Tappan, accusing Lyman Beecher of having neglected to invite the school's only black student to a social function at the school. The charge was not true; the student, a free black man, had received an invitation, but had decided not to attend. Lyman Beecher, however, was put in the uncomfortable position of defending himself to the Lane trustees.

That winter, Weld asked Beecher for permission to hold a public debate on the subject of abolition. Lyman Beecher denied the request, arguing that such a debate would be unwise. Cincinnati was filled with people whose livelihood depended on keeping friendly relations with advocates of slavery. Many were respectable merchants and traders, but the port city was also filled with rough deckhands and drifters who were all too prone to express themselves with violence. The city was also home to a group of free blacks who might become the target of violence if passions were roused and a mob were formed. Mobs had attacked free blacks in other places, and such a tragedy could happen in Cincinnati as well.

Theodore Weld would not listen to reason, however, and Lyman Beecher found himself drawn into a public debate. Every night, for nearly three weeks, the seminary hall was packed with students and citizens eager to hear the arguments on both sides. Beecher drew upon all his eloquence and strength as a speaker to convince the students that gradual emancipation and colonization—not abolition—were the answers to slavery. But Theodore Weld was a gifted, passionate speaker, too, and he was armed with facts about the failure of the American Colonization Society to return no more than a handful of blacks to Africa, despite its valiant efforts. At the end of the debate, the students voted to form the Lane Anti-Slavery Society, and to dedicate themselves to the immediate emancipation of slaves.

As Hatty listened to the debates, she felt confused and conflicted. She understood her father's position, but she could not help agreeing with much of what the students said. She thought it was wonderful when they set up a free school in Cincinnati's black neighborhood and devoted their evenings to teaching former slaves how to read and write. She applauded the students' belief in "social intercourse according to character, irrespective of color,"[3] but she wondered at their wisdom in parading through the streets with their black friends. Hatty had seen the angry looks and heard the sneering comments of people who were outraged by the sight of white divinity students walking arm in arm with black girls. She agreed with her father than such conduct served only to provoke antiblack sentiments among the people of Cincinnati and to fuel their growing anger at the abolitionists.

Lyman Beecher decided that things had gone far enough. He warned the students, "Boys, if you go on this way, you will be overwhelmed."[4] From the pulpit, he preached a rousing sermon in which he reemphasized his own views. When Calvin Stowe gave a similar lecture, Hatty sat in the audience with Eliza Stowe, listening intently. Her father was right about so many things, and here was Calvin Stowe agreeing with him.

But the abolitionist arguments still appealed to her. When Hatty measured Lyman Beecher's arguments against those of the abolitionists, her confusion grew. Who was right? She didn't know. For the time being, she decided not to think about it any longer and to put aside thoughts about slavery.

As the spring term drew to a close, Hatty decided to accompany Mary Dutton on a visit back to New England. She looked forward to the trip. It would be her first visit in two years and, even better, Henry Ward would soon be returning also, to receive his diploma from Amherst. She would be able to attend his graduation in Massachusetts and afterward visit her family and friends in Hartford and Nut Plains. In a flurry of anticipation, Hatty made herself a new dress. When the time came, she and Mary set out by stagecoach on the trip east.

Bubbling with happiness, Hatty wrote long letters to Eliza Stowe, filling them with witty descriptions of people she met along the route. She wrote about "a New Orleans girl . . . with the prettiest language and softest intonations in the world." She described a soft-spoken, well-mannered passenger, "a Mr. Mitchell, the most gentlemanly, obliging man that ever changed his seat forty times a day to please a lady," who was drawn into an argument with a proslavery man until "all [his] philanthropy was roused, and he sprung up all lively and oratorical and gesticulatory and indignant to my heart's content." In a revealing comment, she added, "I like to see a quiet man that can be roused." She went on to describe the majestic scenery along the way, and told Eliza about her almost religious experience on seeing Niagara Falls: "I have seen it and yet live!"[5]

At Amherst, Hatty nearly burst with pride when her handsome, popular brother graduated with honors. After the graduation ceremonies, Hatty and Henry Ward traveled together to Hartford to begin their round of visits. Then came a letter announcing that both Lyman Beecher and Catherine were on their way east and that they planned to spend the summer raising funds and hiring staff for their respective schools.

Lyman Beecher, confident that the members of the Lane Anti-Slavery Society would give him no trouble during the summer, set off on a round of preaching. But while he was exhorting his listeners in New England on the need to save the West for Protestantism, the situation at Lane was growing worse. Some of the students could not afford to return home and were spending the summer in Cincinnati. They were seen around the city with their black friends, and had even invited the blacks to a picnic. A newspaper editorial denounced the students' behavior, and indignation grew to an angry roar.

Alarmed by the situation, a group comprising the more conservative trustees of Lane quickly passed a resolution to abolish the Lane Anti-Slavery Society and to prohibit students from discussing slavery at the school, even among themselves. Then, in an ill-conceived effort to halt public criticism of the seminary, the trustees had the resolution published in a Cincinnati newspaper. Within days, newspapers all over the country reprinted the story. Suddenly, Lane Seminary was famous—not as the "Yale of the West," but as a place in which free speech was prohibited. People quickly concluded that if the seminary oppressed its students and forbid them to speak out against slavery, then Lane Seminary must be a proslavery institution.

Lyman Beecher finally realized that he was faced with a disastrous crisis. He rushed back to Cincinnati, but he was too late. With Theodore Weld as their leader, forty students left the seminary in protest against the oppressive policy that deprived them of their constitutional rights to freedom of speech and association. Eventually, the students enrolled at Oberlin College, a new school in which "free discussion would be tolerated,"[6] and Theodore Weld would go on to become one of the leading spokesmen of the abolitionist movement.

The incident was to leave an indelible stain on the reputation of Lane Seminary. Arthur Tappan, the abolitionist who was the school's chief benefactor, decided to withhold his financial support. With the loss of both students and money, Lane was in ruins. Although Lyman Beecher fought for many years to keep the school alive, the "empire for God" that he had hoped to build in the West was lost in the conflict over slavery.

The problems at Lane would have been disaster enough

for one summer, but August brought further bad news. An outbreak of cholera was sweeping through Cincinnati, leaving sickness and death in its wake. One day, Hatty received news from Calvin Stowe that left her trembling with grief: Eliza Stowe, her dear friend, was dead.

CHAPTER 5

CALVIN STOWE

HATTY WAS crushed by Eliza's death. Eliza Tyler Stowe, beautiful, talented, and popular with all who knew her, was only twenty-five years old when she died of cholera, just two years older than Hatty herself. Like Hatty, Eliza had been the daughter of a well-known clergyman, Dr. Bennett Tyler, and the two young women had shared a pious faith, a love of books and poetry, and a well-developed sense of humor that allowed them to laugh even at themselves. Their friendship had been a source of great pleasure to Hatty. She found it hard to accept that her dear friend was gone, but she put aside her own grief for a few moments to write a compassionate letter of condolence to Eliza's husband, Calvin Stowe.

Calvin Ellis Stowe was a widely respected, brilliant theologian, an expert on Hebraic languages, and a professor of Biblical literature at Lane Seminary where he functioned as Lyman Beecher's right hand. Now, at the age of thirty-two, he found himself a childless widower, overwhelmed by the tragedy of his wife's death.

It was the fall of 1834, and classes had resumed at Lane with a greatly reduced student body. Lyman Beecher needed his friend's support, but Calvin Stowe, absentminded in the best of times, seemed oblivious to the problems at Lane. In fact, he seemed to be drowning in a sea of misery, unable to deal with even the simplest details of daily life. Night after night, he joined the Beechers at their dinner table, seeking consolation for his sorrow.

Hatty's sympathy was aroused by Calvin's helpless condition, and she took pity on the man who had been the husband of her most intimate friend. Every day, Hatty looked after Calvin's needs, making sure that his clothes were clean and mended, that his boots were polished, and that he ate regular meals. Calvin seemed to enjoy talking about Eliza, so Hatty listened sympathetically, hoping that her silent attentions would help him to recover from his loss. As Calvin talked, Hatty found that hearing his recollections of Eliza made it easier to deal with her own bereavement as well. Increasingly dependent on the solace that Hatty afforded him, Calvin Stowe continued his daily visits.

As the weeks and months passed, the friendship between Hatty and Calvin Stowe grew. A short, stout, moon-faced man, Calvin Stowe in no way resembled the romantic ideal of Hatty's youthful imaginings. He was not handsome and poetic like Byron nor was he dashing and reckless like the heroes of Sir Walter Scott's novels. But he had many other, more important qualities that endeared him to Hatty.

Calvin Stowe was a friendly, kindhearted man who understood the problems of the poor and downtrodden from his own experience. Growing up in abject poverty, as he had done in New England, gave him a realistic, practical approach to life. By working hard and saving every penny, he had managed to attend Bowdoin College in Maine, where he was a favorite with his wealthier, more cultured classmates, people such as Henry Wadsworth Longfellow, destined to become a great poet, and Nathaniel Hawthorne, the future novelist. When Calvin was chosen valedictorian of his class, the students congratulated him warmly, and on graduation day, Franklin Pierce, a classmate who would one day become president of the United States, laughingly told Calvin, "You know I only made it because I sat next to you, Stowe."[1]

Hatty's brother, Henry Ward, had taken classes under Calvin Stowe at Lane, and greatly admired both his knowledge and his character. But Calvin's immense learning and intellectual accomplishments did not prevent him from being down-to-earth. He had a fine sense of the absurd and could tell comical stories filled with wry Yankee humor and rustic jokes that sent his listeners into gales of laughter. He was firm in his principles, he envied no man, and he was faithful to his friends. All of these qualities appealed to Hatty and, as the days passed, she found herself growing quite fond of Calvin.

One day, something happened that would draw Hatty and Calvin Stowe even closer together. Hatty, Lyman Beecher, and Calvin Stowe were invited to spend a few days at the home of Reverend Rankin, a Presbyterian minister who lived in Ripley, a river town located a few miles from Cincinnati. Dr. Rankin's house was situated on a high bluff overlooking the Ohio River and the Kentucky shore beyond. Every evening, Dr. Rankin lit a lamp and placed it in a window facing the river. This strange ritual aroused the guests' curiosity, until finally one of them asked Dr. Rankin if there was a meaning to his action. If the truth were known by some people, Dr. Rankin would have found himself in a great deal of trouble. But he trusted his guests, and was soon telling them that the lamp was known as a beacon of freedom to all the slaves across the river. He explained that the slaves knew that if they could escape across the river, they would be given food and shelter in the house with the lamp. Then, they would be helped in reaching the next safe stop on their flight north to Canada.

Hatty, Calvin, and Dr. Beecher had heard rumors about the Underground Railroad. They knew that it was run by brave people who opposed slavery just as much as the outspoken abolitionists, but who chose to show their resistance by quietly helping escaped slaves to gain their freedom. Until now, the three of them had never known anyone who was involved in the clandestine enterprise. They stared in wonder at their host, and urged him to tell them more. Soon, Dr. Rankin was telling them stories about the many slaves who had made their way to his house since he had first lighted the lamp in 1825. One story, however, thrilled his listeners more than all the rest.

It had happened in the month of March several years before. The winter had been bitter cold, and the Ohio River had frozen solid, but an early thaw had caused the ice to crack here and there. One afternoon, across the river in Kentucky, a young slave woman decided to escape from the torments of her cruel master. Clad only in a thin garment, and cradling her baby in her arms, she ran through the woods toward the Ohio. It was night when she reached the river, but beyond it she could see the lamp of freedom shining in the darkness. The river looked dangerous and threatening. She could not tell if the ice would be strong enough to support her weight or if it would break, sending her and her child into the icy water; but desperation drove her on.

Clutching her baby tightly to her breast, she set out over the ice, slipping and falling repeatedly, until she managed finally to struggle across the ice and climb the hill to Dr. Rankin's house. She was soaked to the skin and shivering with cold. Dr. Rankin sat her in front of the fireplace and gave her food and warm, dry clothes. After she had rested a while, he drove her and her baby to the next stop on the Underground Railroad to continue her flight north. After Dr. Rankin returned home later that night, he heard a thunderous roar from the river. The ice was breaking up, and huge chunks were heaving and plunging in the icy current. The poor slave mother had crossed the river just in time.

As Dr. Rankin told the story, Hatty and Calvin pictured the scene vividly in their minds. Later, they talked with one another about the courageous slave mother and their admiration for Dr. Rankin. Hatty, usually shy and quiet in Calvin's presence, found herself speaking out passionately against slavery. Calvin, while echoing her hatred of slavery, revealed a depth of gentleness and compassion that Hatty had never seen in him before. Each realized that the other had been profoundly touched and, in their mutual understanding, they were drawn closer together.

Back in Cincinnati, their friendship ripened into love. Together they attended church and meetings of the Semi-Colon Club. Calvin delivered a series of sermons at Lyman Beecher's church and read some of his papers to the Semi-Colon Club, causing Hatty to remark, "If ever a woman feels proud of her lover it is when she sees him as a successful public speaker."[2] She helped Calvin compile some of his lectures into book form, and she sought his opinions on Catherine's theories of education.

While Hatty and Calvin were wrapped up in their own activities, Dr. Beecher was awash in a sea of trouble. William Lloyd Garrison, the abolitionist, had attacked Lane Seminary in his publication, *The Liberator,* calling it "a Bastille of oppression" and including in the article the ill-advised resolutions of Lane's board of trustees as well as the statement issued by the abolitionist students who had left the school. If that were not enough, Arthur Tappan and a group of New York abolitionists reprinted Garrison's article in pamphlet form and distributed thousands of copies, thereby seriously compromising Lyman Beecher's efforts to increase funding and enrollment for the school. Letters attacking Lane Seminary and Dr. Beecher appeared in Cincinnati newspapers. Then Judge Hall, the editor who had published Hatty's first stories, brought new charges against Lyman Beecher. In an article in the *Western Monthly Magazine,* Hall accused him of "bigotry, intolerance, and incitement of religious hatred against Catholics."[3] Anti-Catholic sentiment was high at the time, and Dr. Beecher had called on his congregation to "save the West from Popery,"[4] so there was some truth to Hall's accusation. Calvin Stowe could no longer stand by while his friend was under siege. He sprang to Lyman Beecher's defense with scores of counterattacking letters, but nothing Calvin said or did could halt the course of events.

The final blow came from Dr. Joshua Lacy Wilson, a

long-standing rival of Beecher's. Dr. Wilson had long dis-agreed with Beecher's teachings on original sin and other fundamental issues. Now that Beecher's prestige was waver-ing because of the antislavery issue, Wilson chose to attack by filing a charge of heresy against Beecher with the Pres-bytery, the church's ruling body. Hatty and Calvin were wor-ried, as indeed all the Beechers were, but Lyman Beecher was confident that he would win.

Dr. Beecher's trial took place in Cincinnati. After days of debating scripture and examining arguments, the church officials reached their verdict: the Reverend Dr. Lyman Beecher was not guilty of heresy. The family breathed a sigh of relief. But their happiness was short-lived.

Mrs. Beecher had been ill for many months. During her husband's trial, her condition had worsened, and now, in July 1835, the second Mrs. Lyman Beecher died. None of Roxanna Beecher's children were overcome by the death of their stepmother. She had always seemed cool and distant to them. But Harriet Porter Beecher left her own three children motherless. James was only seven years old, Thomas was thirteen, and Isabella was fifteen; and they turned to Hatty for comfort. Catherine was away in New England at the time, crusading for reforms in women's education, so Hatty, who was acting head of the Western Female Seminary, took charge of the household. Everyone seemed to be relying on Hatty.

After all the troubles that had fallen on the Beecher household, it was time for a change. In the month following Mrs. Beecher's death, the family gathered for a reunion. Hat-ty's brothers, Edward, George, and William, took time off from their respective churches to make the trip to Cincin-nati, and her sister Mary traveled west as well. They had not been together as a family for several years and, now, here they were, all eleven of Lyman Beecher's remaining children: Catherine, William, Edward, Mary, George, Hatty, Henry Ward, Charles, Isabella, Thomas, and James.

Lyman Beecher was buoyantly happy, and his high spir-its were infectious! Some of his sons were now famous preachers, so he invited them to take turns giving sermons from his pulpit. Full of pride and love for one another, the Beechers prayed and sang and laughed together.

Throughout the days of celebration, Hatty thought of how fortunate she was to belong to such a wonderful family. Left to herself, she would fall into bleak depressions, but here, with her loving family around her, she felt full of confidence and joy.

Calvin Stowe, who had been invited to take part in the reunion, was deeply moved by what he saw. He himself was an only child whose father had died when he was six. He had known little affection from his stern mother and the spinster aunts who had raised him, and he had spent most of his childhood in lonely solitude. His family was grindingly poor and ever since boyhood his life had been filled with hard work and more hard work. Now, as he looked at Hatty, her eyes sparkling with happiness as she laughed and chattered with her close-knit family, Calvin realized what had been missing from his life. No one was surprised when, a few weeks later, Hatty told her family and a few close friends that she and Calvin were engaged.

The wedding took place on January 6, 1836. It was a simple affair, with Lyman Beecher uniting Hatty and Calvin in marriage, and with only Mary Dutton and Hatty's brothers and sisters as witnesses. For weeks before the wedding, Hatty's mind had been filled with turbulent thoughts about her upcoming marriage, but on the day itself, a sense of peace came over her. She was stylishly dressed in a fashionable high-waisted gown, and her hair was arranged in attractive curls.

Shortly before the ceremony, while her family bustled about with last minute details, Hatty found herself with time on her hands. Hatty, being Hatty, sat down calmly at her desk to write a letter to her old friend, Georgiana May.

Well, my dear G., about half an hour more and your old friend, companion, schoolmate, sister, etc., will cease to be Hatty Beecher and change

*to nobody knows who. . . . I have been dreading
and dreading the time, and lying awake all last
week wondering how I should live through this
overwhelming crisis, and lo! it has come and I
feel* nothing at all. *. . . Well, it is really a mercy
to have this entire stupidity come over one at
such a time. I should be crazy to feel as I did
yesterday, or indeed to feel anything at all. But I
inwardly vowed that my last feelings and reflec-
tions on this subject should be yours, and as I
have not got any, it is just as well to tell you
that. Well, here comes Mr. S., so farewell, and
for the last time I subscribe*

                                         *Your own,
                                         H. E. B.*[5]

Three weeks later, Harriet Elizabeth Beecher Stowe wrote to
Georgiana again, reporting that "my husband and self are
now quietly seated by our own fireside, as domestic as any
pair of tame fowl you ever saw. . . . I am tranquil, quiet, and
happy."[6]

THE YOUNG
MRS. STOWE

THE EARLY days of marriage were happy ones for Hatty. She no longer taught at the Western Female Seminary. Away from Catherine's watchful eye, she felt that a burden had been lifted from her shoulders. Instead of being a subservient spinster, Hatty was now a young matron in charge of her own home, "that appointed shrine for women." She was determined to be an ideal New England housewife and to make her home with Calvin a model of neatness, cleanliness, and peace. She threw herself periodically into energetic bouts of scrubbing, washing, and baking. But just as often, she found herself wandering around the house in an abstracted mood, while her plans for order and accomplishment went out the window. Hatty learned things about herself that she had never known before: she was apt to be disorganized and she did not like housework.

Hatty also learned some things about Calvin that she had overlooked before their wedding. Like herself, her husband was subject to fits of moodiness and depression, but his were deeper and lasted longer than her own. He sometimes had strange visions, peopled with illusory characters, that sent an eerie chill up her spine when he spoke to her about them. And when he felt unable to cope with problems,

Calvin developed imaginary illnesses. He would go to bed and stay there for days at a time. When it came to doing things around the house, Calvin was of no help. He was clumsy and uncoordinated, and Hatty realized that if she wanted to hang curtains, move furniture, or build a cupboard, she was better off doing it herself. Calvin's most disappointing trait, however, was his inability to deal with the practical realities of daily life. Despite his mental brilliance, he seemed unable to plan his career or to make economic decisions. Hatty realized that she would have to pay more attention to their financial affairs.

A few months after the wedding, Calvin was appointed by the state of Ohio to make a study of European school systems with a view to improving the public schools in the United States. "He sails the first of May!" she wrote to Georgiana, adding that she intended to see Calvin off when his ship sailed from New York and, after he was gone, to visit family and friends. But as the day for Calvin's departure grew closer, Hatty had to change her plans. She discovered that she was pregnant; so, instead of vacationing in New England, Hatty would stay in her father's house while Calvin was away.

Calvin would be gone for nearly a year, and Hatty would miss him dreadfully. Knowing that he would miss her, too, she put aside her own feelings to write him a cheerful letter that he could open and read after he was at sea.

> *Now, my dear, that you are gone where you are*
> *out of the reach of my care, advice, and good*
> *management, it is fitting that you should have*
> *something under my hand and seal for your*
> *comfort . . . dear one, you must give more way*
> *to hope than memory. You are going to a new*
> *scene now, and one that I hope will be full of*
> *enjoyment to you. I want you to take the good of*
> *it. Only think of all you expect to see: the great*
> *libraries and beautiful paintings, fine churches . . .*
> *My dear, I wish I were a man in your place; if I*
> *wouldn't have a grand time!*[1]

While Calvin was in Europe, Hatty kept up a daily schedule of writing. She wrote short stories and articles for publication in the *Western Monthly Magazine* and the *New York Evangelist,* and she kept a daily journal, filled with news and observations, which she mailed to Calvin once a month. She also helped her brother, Henry Ward, who was serving temporarily as the editor of the *Journal,* a small daily newspaper, while the paper's regular editor was accompanying Lyman Beecher on a trip to New England.

Now twenty-three years old, Henry Ward Beecher was an outgoing, confident young man. Eager to speak his mind publicly, he wrote stirring editorials for the paper. Since he and Hatty had always been very close, he invited his favorite sister to write for the newspaper, too. And he asked Charles to contribute articles on his favorite subject, music. For a time, at least, the *Journal* would be a Beecher newspaper.

The summer of 1836 turned out to be more exciting than Hatty and Henry Ward anticipated. It marked the arrival in Cincinnati of a lawyer named James G. Birney. Birney was a former slave owner from Alabama, who had become a radical abolitionist. He had freed his slaves and founded an antislavery newspaper called *The Philanthropist.* After encountering troubles elsewhere, he decided to publish his paper in Cincinnati where he was joined in his efforts by a young doctor named Gamaliel Bailey.

Birney and his newspaper were not welcomed in Cincinnati. A mass meeting was held to denounce him and all abolitionists, but Birney ignored the growing tensions and continued to publish provocative articles against slavery. During that summer of 1836, hundreds of southerners arrived in the city to celebrate the inauguration of a railroad link between Cincinnati and the South. As the days passed, the mutterings against Birney grew into violent shouting, and on a hot July night, a proslavery mob broke into his office and attacked the presses on which *The Philanthropist* was printed.

Henry Ward fired off a piece condemning the mob's actions and defending freedom of speech and of the press.

Hatty quickly wrote a companion piece designed to draw attention to Henry's long editorial. Hatty and Henry Ward hoped that Birney would not be frightened away. They were not disappointed. The courageous Birney continued to publish his paper.

But anger and threats of violence mounted. At a citywide meeting, a group of Cincinnati's most influential citizens agreed to put a stop to Birney and his newspaper. Henry Ward denounced the resolution in a stirring editorial, and Hatty, writing to Calvin, said

> *I wish father were at home to preach a sermon to his church, for many of its members do not frown on these things as they ought. . . . The mob madness is certainly upon this city when men of sense and standing will pass resolutions approving in so many words of things done contrary to law. . . . Mr. Hammond (editor of the* Gazette) *in a very dignified and judicious manner has condemned the whole thing, and Henry has opposed, but otherwise the papers have either been silent or in favor of mobs.*[2]

Nothing could stop the bitter antiabolitionist reactionaries as, once again, the mob gathered. Having failed to find Birney himself, they demolished his office, smashed his printing press, and threw it in the river. They then went on a rampage, destroying houses of "inoffensive and respectable blacks," and threatening to attack Lane Seminary and the offices of the *Gazette* and the *Journal.* The following evening, Hatty trembled with fear and pride as she watched Henry Ward strap a pistol to his side and ride off into the night. Along with a group of other responsible citizens, he finally dispersed the mob after two days of rioting.

Years later, Hatty recalled, "I saw for the first time clearly that the institution of slavery was incapable of defense. . . . That summer and fall opened my eyes to the real nature of slavery as they had never been opened before."[3] Despite these events, neither Hatty nor Henry Ward was convinced that the abolitionists were right. Nevertheless, they were shocked by the way a gentle man like Birney had been treated for voicing his belief that slaves should be freed. "It does seem to me," Hatty wrote, "that there needs to be an *intermediate* society. If not, as light increases, all the excesses of the abolition party will not prevent humane and conscientious men from joining it. . . . No one can have the system of slavery brought before him without an irrepressible desire to *do* something, and what is there to be done?"[4] For the time being, however, Hatty had no answers. It was something she would have to think about long and hard.

But Hatty's attention was soon shifted to domestic issues when, a few weeks after the riots, Lyman Beecher returned home, bringing with him a new wife. Lydia Jackson Beecher was a pleasant, agreeable widow with two children from her former marriage. If Lyman Beecher was happy, so were his children. Lydia Jackson Beecher soon fit in with the rest of the household.

The excitement of having a new stepmother was diminished by another event that was to change Hatty's life. The trees had just begun to don their brilliant fall colors when, on September 26, 1836, Hatty gave birth to not one but two baby girls. Calvin was still away in Europe, so Hatty named one baby Eliza Tyler and the other Isabella. When Calvin came home four months later, he declared that if one child was to be named for his dead wife, Eliza, the other must be named for his beloved Hatty. So, at Calvin's insistence, Isabella was renamed Harriet Beecher.

Now with a young family to care for, Hatty and Calvin struggled to make ends meet. Calvin set to work. He prepared a report on European schools, emphasizing the excellence of schools in Prussia, and delivered it to the governor of Ohio in Columbus. He wrote to Hatty, "For my year's work in this matter I am to receive $500."[5] It wasn't much, but it would have to do.

When they were married, Hatty's "dowry" had consisted of eleven dollars' worth of dishes. Calvin had brought a load of books with him. Together, they lived in a small rented house, owned only a few sticks of furniture, and were too poor to afford more. In 1837, a financial crisis threw the nation into an economic depression. Contributions to Lane Seminary all but dried up, and Calvin learned that he was to receive only a portion of his small salary.

Before the advent of electricity and the invention of labor-saving appliances, housework was drudgery, pure and simple. For instance, before electric washing machines and dryers became available, washing the laundry was an all-day affair. The process began by building a fire either in the stove or outdoors, drawing water from a well, and then heating it in a large kettle or washtub. Then the laundry was boiled. Homemade soap was used to scrub the clothes and linens by hand. Next, more water had to be drawn to rinse the laundry. When it was finally clean, the laundry had to be squeezed out by hand and then hung outdoors on a line to dry. Because every household task, from cooking to cleaning, involved a mountain of hard, physical labor, even families of modest means employed servants to help the woman of the house.

The Stowes, however, were too poor to afford hired help, so Hatty took care of the twins and did all the cooking and housework herself. Tired as she was, Hatty did not give up writing; the need to put her thoughts and feelings on paper had become a compulsive habit. Beyond that, the Stowes desperately needed whatever money she could earn from writing. She often found herself letting the dust gather and the laundry pile high while she scribbled away on long sheets of cheap paper. Her stories and articles found their way into print, and eventually she was able to use some of her earnings to hire a girl to help with the housework. But late in the spring of 1837, Hatty discovered that she was pregnant again and, despite the hired girl's help, she was exhausted. Alarmed by the state of Hatty's health, Calvin insisted that she take a vacation.

Hatty took the twins and went off for a brief visit to her brother William in Putnam, Ohio. William, his wife, and many of their friends had been converted to abolitionism and, once again, Hatty was drawn into discussions about slavery. She thoughtfully considered William's powerful argument that slavery was a sin and that, as such, it had to be fought against—not some time in the future, but now. Hatty found herself facing a personal moral dilemma. She knew deep in her heart that the abolitionists were right, but she also knew, from her experiences in Cincinnati, that slave owners would not give up without a fierce struggle. Like her father, she believed that the measures advocated by the abolitionists were sure to provoke violence, and Hatty hated violence. Surely, she thought, if the North and South understood one another better, violence might be avoided. If efforts to educate both sides failed, only then might more drastic measures be justified.

No sooner did Hatty return home to Cincinnati than terrible news arrived from Illinois, where her brother Edward was a minister. Edward had been aiding a man named Dr. Elijah Lovejoy who, like Birney in Cincinnati, had been publishing a fiery abolitionist newspaper. Just as in Cincinnati, a mob stormed Lovejoy's office and destroyed his press. The news from Alton, Illinois, reported that Elijah Lovejoy had been killed and, even worse, that Edward Beecher had been murdered, too.

The Beechers were horrified and distraught. Their own dear Edward had joined the ranks of martyrs in the struggle over slavery. A few days later, they received word that a mistake had been made. It was true that Edward had been present when the mob had attacked Lovejoy, but Edward's life had been spared. He was alive and unhurt. Hatty thanked God for his deliverance, but the event left her deeply shaken. The violence surrounding the question of slavery had struck too close to home.

But once again, Hatty's attention was diverted by more immediate concerns. On January 14, 1838, her third child,

Henry Ellis, was born. The twins, now fifteen months old, had just begun to walk and talk and, with a new infant to care for, Hatty had little time for anything else. She wrote to Georgiana May,

> *How changed I am . . . the mother of three children! . . . Indeed, my dear, I am but a mere drudge with few ideas beyond babies and housekeeping. . . . I suppose I am a dolefully uninteresting person at present, but I hope I shall grow young again one of these days, for it seems to me that matters cannot always stand exactly as they do now . . . this marriage is—yes, I will speak well of it, after all; for when I can stop and think long enough to discriminate my head from my heels, I must say that I think myself a fortunate woman both in husband and children. My children I would not change for all the ease, leisure, and pleasure that I could have without them.*[6]

Although her children and housekeeping consumed her days, the problem of slavery continued to haunt Hatty. This time, the problem showed its face in her own kitchen. The young black girl whom Hatty had hired to help with the housework was in trouble. When Hatty hired her, the girl had claimed that she was free. Then, one evening, she rushed into the house, breathless and frightened. Barely stopping to catch her breath, she tearfully blurted out the truth: she had lied. She was not free; she had escaped from bondage in Kentucky, and now her master was in Cincinnati looking for her. Would Dr. and Mrs. Stowe help her?

Calvin didn't know what to do, so Hatty sent for Henry Ward. Together, they made hurried plans to send the girl away to a safe place. Late that night, Henry Ward and Calvin armed themselves. Then they hid the girl in the back of a wagon and drove off on dark country roads to the farm of a man who sheltered fugitive slaves. Hatty couldn't sleep. Helping runaway slaves was illegal and risky. She expected at any moment to hear a knock at the door or the pounding hooves of horses in hot pursuit. Throughout the long night, she paced the floor, listening intently to every sound until, toward dawn, Calvin and Henry Ward returned safely. Hatty was frightened and worried, but what else could a decent Christian do? It was wrong for one human being to own another as property.

Throughout the early years of their marriage, poverty plagued the Stowes, as it would for many years to come. The situation at Lane Seminary was getting worse; only ten students showed up for the fall term in 1838, and both Lyman Beecher and Calvin worried that Lane might be forced to shut its doors. Calvin, as he always did in times of crisis, went to bed and stayed there. While Hatty pampered him with hot soup and cups of tea, Calvin raved hopelessly about their situation. Hatty listened sympathetically to his complaints and fears, and tried to raise his spirits by telling him that he was a fine man and a famous scholar. She had discovered that, while Calvin ran away from problems, she had an inner strength that compelled her to stand and fight.

Despite her domestic problems, Hatty managed somehow to find time each day to write. She was determined that the Stowes would not starve or go homeless. They would *not* go to the poorhouse, not if she could help it. She churned out stories and articles for several publications and, within a few months, payments for them began to trickle in. Feeling hopeful about the future, she wrote to Mary Dutton,

> *I have about three hours per day in writing: and*
> *if you see my name coming out everywhere, you*
> *may be sure of one thing—that I do it for the*
> *pay. . . . I have determined not to be a mere do-*
> *mestic slave, without even the leisure to excel in*
> *my duties. I mean to have money enough to have*
> *my house kept in the best manner and yet to have*
> *time for reflection and that preparation for the edu-*
> *cation of my children that every mother needs.*[7]

In the meantime, Lyman Beecher was fighting for the survival of Lane Seminary and managed to recruit additional students for the school. Appearing at the Stowes' house one day, he marched into the bedroom and thundered at his son-in-law, "Get up, Stowe. I've brought ye twelve students. Get up and wash and eat bread, and prepare to have a good class."[8] Calvin moaned and groaned, but did as he was told. For a while, at least, Lane Seminary would remain open.

Between the demands of children, husband, and domestic tasks, it is amazing that Hatty was able to write at all. A friend of hers at the time described how she managed to juggle all the distractions. He recalled how he walked in on her one day, saying, "Come Harriet . . . where is that piece for the *Souvenir* which I promised the editor I would get from you and send on next week? You have only this one day left to finish it, and have it I must." Hatty protested that the baby was teething, that she had baking and housecleaning to attend to, that "It is really out of the question." Her friend insisted: " 'You know you can write anywhere and anyhow. Just take your seat at the kitchen table. . . . Two dollars a page, my dear, and you can write a page in fifteen minutes . . . consider the economy of the thing.' I carried my point. In ten minutes she was seated; a table with flour, rolling pin, ginger, and lard on one side, a dresser with eggs, pork and beans, and various cooking utensils on the other, near her an oven heating, and beside her a dark-skinned nymph, waiting orders."[9]

The story that was due concerned a tearful romance and, between interruptions by the children and giving instructions to the hired girl, Hatty dictated the conclusion as her friend wrote it down.

> Hatty: " 'I know my duty to my children. I see the hour must come. You must take them, Henry; they are my last earthly comfort.' "
> Hired Girl: "Ma'am, what shall I do with these egg-shells and all this truck here?"

Hatty: "Put them in the pail by you."
Friend: " 'They are my last earthly comfort.
What next?' "
Hatty: " 'You must take them away. I may
be—perhaps it must *be—that I shall soon follow,*
but the breaking heart of a wife still pleads, "a little
longer, a little longer." ' "
Hired Girl: "How much longer must the gin-
gerbread stay in?"
Hatty: "Five minutes."
Friend, laughing, "A little longer, a little
longer."[10]

They went on in this manner until, between cooking, nursing, and laughing, the story was finally finished.

During this period, Hatty turned out scores of stories and articles. She wrote romantic fiction, set in New England, that was published in prestigious magazines such as *Godey's Lady's Book.* Her nonfiction pieces dealt with topics ranging from the evils of alcohol and the shameful starvation wages paid by wealthy women to their maids and seamstresses, to articles on keeping the Sabbath, the servant problem, and a piece on her brother, Henry Ward, who was gaining a reputation as a silver-tongued preacher second to none.

Hatty was working hard, and her efforts were paying off. She was even able to save a little money with which she hoped to buy some much-needed furniture. When Calvin was invited to deliver a Phi Beta Kappa oration at Dartmouth College in June of 1839, Hatty decided to accompany him. Away from Cincinnati, their spirits rose. They visited with family and friends, and they enjoyed each other's company as they had not been able to do for some time. When they returned to Cincinnati, both Hatty and Calvin were in a happy, cheerful mood. Hatty set to work immediately on a new series of New England stories. Then, late in 1839, she discovered that she was pregnant once again.

CHAPTER 7

POVERTY, SICKNESS, AND SORROW

THROUGHOUT THE first years of her marriage to Calvin, Hatty never lost her sense of humor or her fierce determination. She was happier than she had ever been before, and she enjoyed her role as wife and mother. Her children, especially, were a constant source of delight. She was quick to laugh at the antics of the three little "mischiefs," and she was always ready to see the humor in events around her.

Like her father, Hatty wasted no time looking back at or regretting things that could not be changed. She was a small, delicate woman but, like all the Beechers, she was a strongwilled realist. Whenever Calvin felt like running away from problems, Hatty found that her determination to stand and fight only increased. She would take charge, drawing on her surprising reservoir of strength and resolution to rescue Calvin from his dark moods and to keep the family going.

In the past, Hatty had often sought the advice and opinions of her brothers and sister Catherine. With their help, she had come to terms with her religious doubts and resolved at last to live an "external" life and to submit to God's will in all things. But, as the decade of the 1840s neared, her brothers no longer lived nearby. Henry Ward had married and moved to Indiana where he was the pastor of a small church; William and George were pastors in New York; Edward headed a congregation in Boston; and Charles, meshed in his own struggle with religious doubts, was working as a cotton broker in New Orleans. As her family dispersed, Hatty relied more and more on her own good sense to work through whatever problems lay in her path.

As the new year approached, Hatty looked toward the future with a head full of optimistic dreams. She could not foresee that 1840 would usher in a decade of hardships and trials that were to test her strength and endurance to their limits.

Hatty's long ordeal began when her fourth child, a son, was born in May 1840. He was named Frederick William in honor of the Prussian king, "old Fritz," whom Calvin admired and whom he had met while studying school systems in Europe. It was a difficult pregnancy for Hatty, and the bouts of illness that plagued her through the long months continued after the baby was born. Much of the time she felt too sick to write. In December 1840, she described her troubles in a letter to Georgiana May : "my dear little Frederick was born, and for two months more I was confined to my bed. . . . For a year I have held the pen only to write an occasional business letter such as could not be neglected."[1]

Although she was writing nothing new, Hatty's previously published stories were gaining a modest popularity. When a New York publishing firm sent a letter suggesting that her New England stories be collected in book form, Hatty was delighted that her "scribblings" were receiving recognition. Full of excitement, she traveled to New York City in the spring of 1842. There she met with the publishers, the Harper brothers, who agreed to produce a collection of her stories in a book entitled *The Mayflower: Sketches of Scenes and Characters among the Descendants of the Pilgrims*. The advance royalty payment was small—only one hundred dollars—but, she wrote to Calvin, "the publisher says the book will sell, and . . . I shall make something on it."[2] She also visited the editors of several magazines who promised good payment for anything she chose to write. Hatty reported the good news in another letter to Calvin, adding, "My dear, if I choose to be a literary lady, I have, I think, as good a chance of making a profit by it as anyone I know of. But . . . I have my doubts whether I shall be able to do so."[3]

Despite his constant complaints about troubles, both real and imagined, Calvin Stowe was a kind, generous man who had great faith in his remarkable wife, and unbounded admiration for the entire Beecher family. To shore up her confidence, he replied, "My dear, you must be a literary woman. It is so written in the book of fate. Make all your calculations accordingly. . . . Drop the E. out of your name. . . . Write yourself fully and always Harriet Beecher Stowe, which is a name euphonious, flowing, and full of meaning." Then, in an outburst of affection, Calvin continued, "And now, my dear wife, I want you to come home as quick as you can. The fact is I cannot live without you, and if we were not so prodigious poor I would come for you at once. There is no woman like you in this wide world."[4]

Calvin's feelings for Hatty were echoed in her reply to him: "I did not know till I came away how much I was dependent upon you. . . . If you were not already my dearly loved husband I should certainly fall in love with you."[5]

There can be no doubt that Calvin and Hatty were deeply in love with one another. When problems weighed him down, Calvin knew that he could always rely on Hatty's support. And when Hatty's confidence wavered, Calvin's encouragement and approval spurred her on. She made her "calculations" and came to a decision: "If I am to write, I must have a room to myself, which shall be *my* room." Until that time, she had done all of her writing while sitting at the kitchen table and, as she explained to Calvin,

> *All last winter I felt the need of some place*
> *where I could go and be quiet . . . there was all*
> *the setting of tables, and clearing up of tables,*

and dressing and washing of children, and ev-
erything else going on, and the constant falling
of soot and coal dust on everything in the
room. . . . Then if I came into the parlor where
you were I felt as if I were interrupting you, and
you know you sometimes thought so too."[6]

In his reply, Calvin assured Hatty that her wish would be
granted: she would have a room of her own.

Hatty's mind was filled with ambitious ideas. As soon as
she returned to Cincinnati, she set to work arranging furniture and flowering plants in the room she had chosen for her
study. At last she had some peace and quiet and, for a few
months, she was able to maintain her new schedule of writing several hours a day. Working in the solitude of her own
special room, she found that her writing was going well. But
her new happiness was short-lived.

During the winter of 1842, a typhoid fever epidemic
broke out in Cincinnati. Many students at Lane Seminary fell
ill, and Lyman Beecher's house was used as a hospital. "It
was a season of sickness and gloom,"[7] Hatty wrote, recalling
how the Beecher family had nursed the sick and dying. She
hoped that she would soon be able to return to a full schedule of writing, but her plans fell apart. Hatty discovered that
she was pregnant once again.

It was not an easy pregnancy. As the weeks passed,
Hatty's strength seemed to ebb away. The twins, Eliza and
Harriet, were now seven years old, Henry Ellis was five, and
Frederick was three. They were bright, lively children, and
they constantly sought her attention. Hatty tried to keep up
with the cooking, cleaning, washing, and sewing while caring
for her children, but the strain was beginning to show. While
visiting Hatty one day, Catherine Beecher found her sister
nervous and depressed. She expressed her hope that Hatty
would be able to have "an interval of rest," but there seemed
to be no relief in sight.

A small ray of happiness brightened Hatty's spirits when

she received the first copy of her book, *The Mayflower.* It contained fifteen stories whose themes foreshadowed much of her later writing. Among them were a few romances such as "Love versus Law," a rambling tale about a New England Romeo and his Juliet. Pathetic death scenes, which were so appealing to the sentimentality of nineteenth-century readers, appeared in "Uncle Tim" and "Little Edward." But the book also contained stories that reflected the Beecher zeal for reform. "Let Every Man Mind his own Business," (a story especially pleasing to Lyman Beecher), was Hatty's contribution to the temperance crusade; "The Sabbath" showed the need for special church services for children; and "The Seamstress" called for better treatment of working-class people.

Hatty was pleased with the book, and with the compliments she received from her family and friends. The praise was well deserved; it was a fine book, filled with humor and shrewd insights. But Hatty's brief moment in the sun was soon overshadowed by a tragic event.

In July 1843, she received a letter from Rochester, New York, that sent her tumbling into the depths of depression. While shooting at birds that were destroying the fruit on a tree in his garden, her brother, the Reverend George Beecher, had accidentally killed himself when his double-barreled gun misfired. The suddenness of George's death stunned Hatty. Despite the consolations offered by her religious faith, Hatty found it difficult to accept the fact that her cheerful, talented brother was dead.

In August 1843, barely a month after George's death, Hatty gave birth to her fifth child, a daughter, who was named Georgiana May in honor of her friend. The baby was tiny and weak, and cried constantly. As she fought to keep the child alive, Hatty felt "haunted and pursued by care that seemed to drink my life blood."[8] Although her valiant efforts to save little Georgiana were successful, her own health collapsed and she became so ill that she was forced again to remain in bed for months. Her dream of becoming "a literary lady" lay in ruins.

While Hatty fought to regain her health, another enemy gathered strength. Throughout their marriage, the Stowes had been poor, but in the fall of 1843, their economic situation became desperate. Poverty—hard poverty—laid siege to the household. Lane Seminary, struggling to stay open, could pay Calvin only half of his annual teaching salary of twelve hundred dollars. The Stowes were forced to eke out their existence on a meager six hundred dollars. Hatty wrote to Georgiana May, "Our straits for money this year are unparalleled even in our annals." [9]

During the next few years, Hatty was often left alone with the children while Calvin went off on fund-raising trips for Lane. Tortured by painful headaches and eye problems, and plagued by constant worries, she nevertheless forced herself to write, often working far into the night, in hopes of earning a few dollars.

Among the stories Hatty wrote at this time was "Immediate Emancipation," published in 1845. About a slave who is well treated by his master but who lives in terror that someday he will be sold to pay his master's debts, the story was inspired by a scene she had witnessed one day near the waterfront. Hatty had watched a slave family being sold. The mother was purchased by one man, the father by another buyer; their little girl cried bitterly as her parents were led away. Outraged by this cruelty and injustice, Hatty managed to borrow the money to purchase the child and reunite her with her mother.

Several years earlier, Hatty had accepted Lyman Beecher's moderate views about slavery. But, by the mid-1840s, she, along with her brothers Edward and Henry Ward, had become a staunch abolitionist. The constant spectacle of suffering around her caused her to change her mind. She met former slaves who regaled her with heartbreaking stories. A woman who had been a slave told Hatty that all her children had been fathered by her former master. Compassion welled up in Hatty's heart when the woman remarked, "You know, Mrs. Stowe, slave women cannot help themselves."[10] From other former slaves, Hatty learned about the beatings and

starvation that were all too common on southern plantations. When a group of former slaves settled on property
owned by Lane Seminary, Hatty discovered that their children could neither read nor write. She decided to teach them
herself, although the hours spent with the children robbed
her of precious time.

Hatty sometimes felt like a slave herself, living as she
did; when she took a hard look at her life, she saw only an
overworked housewife and mother, the wife of a brilliant but
impractical clergyman, and a little-known writer of minor
stories. Her days were filled with noisy children, dirty dishes,
piles of laundry, and endless chores. Tired and worried all
the time, she could get no rest, but despite her bad health,
she tried desperately to do everything. Finally, the constant
strain took its toll, leaving her on the brink of physical and
nervous collapse.

During one of Calvin's trips away from home, she wrote
to him,

> *It is a dark, sloppy, rainy, muddy, disagreeable
> day, and I have been working hard (for me) in
> the kitchen . . . I am sick of the smell of sour
> milk, and sour meat, and sour everything, and
> then the clothes will not dry, and no wet thing
> does, and everything smells mouldy. . . . I feel no
> life, no energy, no appetite . . . I suffer with sen-
> sible distress in the brain. . . . When the brain
> gives out, as mine often does, and one cannot
> think or remember anything, then what is to be
> done?*[11]

It was clear to Calvin that something had to be done for his
ailing wife. When Hatty wrote to him about a spa in Brattleboro, Vermont, where mineral water baths were reputed to
cure people of many mysterious diseases, Calvin answered
saying that he wished they had money enough to send her.
Echoing Lyman Beecher's assurance that the Lord would

always provide, Hatty replied, "If God wills, I go . . . if He sees it is really best He will doubtless help me."[12] Then, almost miraculously, the necessary funds were donated to Calvin by people who had learned of Hatty's illness.

In March 1846, Hatty journeyed to Vermont in the company of her sisters Catherine and Mary. She stayed for more than a year, undergoing a rigorous regimen of baths, special diets, and exercise. The daily water-cure was a tiresome process, but life at the Brattleboro Sanitarium was also enjoyable. The spa was a fashionable place, and Hatty met many socially prominent people at the pleasant dances and entertainments that were held there during the evenings. Freed from household drudgery and the demands of her family, Hatty began to relax and enjoy herself.

As her health gradually improved, she felt guilty about leaving Calvin behind in Cincinnati where, left alone to cope with all the burdens, he dragged through the long days, teaching at Lane and caring for the children. "I really pity you in having such a wife," Hatty wrote, "I feel as if I had been only a hindrance to you instead of a help."[13] She cautioned Calvin to take care of himself, warning him that "there is no use my trying to get well, if you in the meantime are going to run yourself down," and begging him for patience, "for this cannot last forever . . . bear it like the toothache, or a driving rain, or anything else that you cannot escape."[14]

At last, after fourteen months in Vermont, Hatty was well enough to return home to her five children and her beleaguered husband. When she arrived in Cincinnati in May 1847, the children swarmed around her, and Calvin, whose endurance was nearly at an end, welcomed her with open arms. She felt better than she had in years, but her new well being was not to last. Soon after her return, Hatty found herself pregnant again. Then the eye problems and headaches returned. She found it almost impossible to write. It seemed to Hatty as though she had never been away at all.

Hatty was thirty-six years old when her sixth child, a boy named Samuel Charles, was born in January 1848.

Calvin, whose imaginary illnesses had developed into real ones during Hatty's absence, could offer little help. He wished that he, too, might spend some time at the spa in Vermont. Hatty prayed fervently that God would once again provide the means.

As if in answer to Hatty's prayers, the financial problems of Lane Seminary were suddenly resolved. Someone had discovered that the hills on which the seminary stood were ideal for planting vineyards. Lyman Beecher, who had seen no contradiction in preaching against liquor while standing above a church basement filled with rum, now saw no problem in planting wine-producing grapes on seminary land. By 1848, revenues from the vineyards began to pour in and Lyman Beecher no longer had to rely on contributions to keep Lane Seminary going. Calvin would receive his full salary. Even better, the seminary granted Dr. Stowe a full year's leave.

In June 1848, Calvin lost no time in setting out for Vermont and leaving Hatty alone with their six children. Nearly all of Calvin's salary would be needed to pay for his expenses, so Hatty would have to find a way to support her children and herself.

Almost overnight, Hatty's terrible headaches and eye pains disappeared. She bubbled with more energy and optimism than she had felt in years, and she laid plans to keep her family afloat financially. Her first step was to crowd the children and herself into a few rooms of the house, and to rent the newly vacant rooms to boarders. With the help of one servant, she managed to keep the household running smoothly.

She had sacrificed her special writing room, so every night, after the children were tucked in bed, Hatty sat down at her old kitchen table to write. There, in the dim glow of an oil lamp, she wrote at a furious pace. The pile of stories and articles grew, and each page that flowed from her pen translated into much-needed money.

Hatty's stories, which dealt mainly with domestic and romantic themes, reflected nothing of the events that shook the nation in the 1840s. Texas had revolted against Mexico and, after achieving independence, had joined the United States. Through its own war with Mexico, the United States acquired territories that reached the shores of the Pacific Ocean. The discovery of gold in the newly acquired lands had sent thousands of people streaming westward in the California Gold Rush. Weighed down by her own concerns, Hatty seemed oblivious to the upheavals in the world around her.

Slavery was the only national issue that disturbed Hatty—and it still disturbed her greatly. From her many black acquaintances, she learned about their great hunger for freedom. She had aided fugitives and had helped to ransom slaves. She knew of their terrible sufferings, the ruthless separations of their families, and the doom that faced those who were sold "down South." But what could one person do to fight the laws that made slavery legal? What could a woman, the mother of six children, do to defeat the great political and economic powers that held the system firmly in place?

Feeling poor and powerless herself, Hatty confined her writing to pieces that would sell—stories and articles that would help to feed her family and keep them safe. She wrote to Georgiana, "I wish you could see me with my flock all around me. They sum up my cares. . . . They are my work, over which I fear and tremble."[15]

Although Hatty worked feverishly to provide for her children, nothing she did could keep her family safe forever. Calvin was still away in Vermont when a new outbreak of Asiatic cholera swept through Cincinnati in the summer of 1849. Doctors had little understanding of the disease and thought it was spread through the air by a thin mist, or "miasma." To combat the miasma, coal fires were lighted on every street corner, filling the humid summer air with suffocating clouds of thick, black smoke. The polluted air did nothing to halt the disease and, as the days passed, the number of deaths increased. The streets echoed with the rumble of hearses as they rolled ominously toward the cemeteries.

Calvin was filled with anxiety about his family and wanted to return home, but Hatty implored him to remain in Vermont. "As regards to your coming home," she wrote to him in June, "I am decidedly against it." To do so, she said, "would be extremely dangerous." She reported that so many people were dying that "hearse drivers have scarce been allowed to unharness their horses, while furniture carts and common vehicles are often employed for the removal of the dead."[16] On one day alone, more than one hundred twenty funerals had rolled somberly past the Stowe house.

For a while, it seemed as though Hatty's home might be spared from the ravages of the plague. But that was not to be. The household's first victim was Aunt Frankie, the old black woman who helped with the laundry. Hatty followed the body to the graveyard to make sure that the old woman was given a decent Christian burial. Next, the children's little dog was seized with fits and died within half an hour.

Then, on July 10, the baby, Samuel Charles, fell ill. Hatty carried him to a doctor who advised a course of treatment, but warned her that the child might suffer a "dropsy of the brain."[17] With a heavy heart, Hatty returned home. She followed the doctor's orders and for a few days it seemed as though the baby would recover. But then, on July 23, she wrote to Calvin, "At last, my dear, the hand of the Lord hath touched us. We have been watching all day by the dying bed of little Charley, who is gradually sinking. . . . Do not return. All will be over before you could possibly get here, and the epidemic is now said by the physicians to prove fatal to every new case."[18]

On July 29, Hatty had to brush aside her tears to write to Calvin once again:

*My dear Husband,—at last it is over and our
dear little one is gone from us. He is now among
the blessed. My Charley—my beautiful, loving,
gladsome baby, so loving, so sweet, so full of life
and hope and strength—now lies shrouded, pale*

*and cold, in the room below. Never was he any-
thing to me but a comfort. He has been my pride
and joy. Many a heartache has he cured for me.
Many an anxious night have I held him to my
bosom and felt the sorrow and loneliness pass
out of me with the touch of his little warm hands.
Yet I have just seen him in his death agony,
looked on his imploring face when I could not
help nor soothe nor do one thing, not one, to
mitigate his cruel suffering, do nothing but pray
in my anguish that he might die soon. I write as
though there were no sorrow like my sorrow, yet
there has been in this city, as in the land of
Egypt, scarce a house without its dead. This
heart-break, this anguish, has been everywhere,
and when it will end God alone knows.*[19]

Hatty was alone when she watched her baby die. And she
had to bury him alone. For many days after the funeral, she
wandered aimlessly around the house, scarcely aware that
the epidemic had abated and that life in the city was returning to normal. She did not know it yet, but her years of
hardship were nearly over. They were years that might have
crushed the spirit of a lesser person, but Hatty's determination and courage had not allowed her to give in. Like the
trials and tribulations sent by God to test the faith and endurance of Job, Hatty's troubles had only strengthened her.
Her spirit was like a strong, sharp blade of steel, forged in
the fires of circumstance and tempered by adversity.

At last, in September 1849, Calvin returned to Cincinnati, looking healthy and fit. He put his arms around the
small, frail, grief-stricken woman who was his wife, and told
her the good news. He had accepted the offer of a profes-
sorship at Bowdoin College in Brunswick, Maine. He would
be receiving a better salary, and the Stowes would return to
their beloved New England. The years of suffering were over.
Hatty's exile in the West was at an end.

CHAPTER 8

"I WILL WRITE THAT THING!"

IN 1850, AS the Stowes were planning to retrace their steps east, the rest of the nation was looking westward. Back in 1811 when Hatty was born, the United States comprised seventeen states. But by mid-century, the nation had stretched from coast to coast, reaching its continental limits, and fulfilling what some people called the nation's "manifest destiny."[1] The land was there, it was there to be taken, and taken it was. Whether it was taken by treaty, by force, or by chicanery mattered little to most people.

What did matter, however, was whether or not slavery would be permitted in the two million square miles west of the Mississippi River. Northerners were anxious to keep the new territories free of slavery, but southerners argued that abandoning slavery would result in economic ruin and social chaos. Slavery, they said, was not the evil institution denounced by ignorant Yankees. On the contrary, they argued, it kept the black race from heathen barbarism, it ensured continued peace and prosperity, and, in any case, it was protected by constitutional guarantees governing the ownership of private property.

In 1820, Congress had tried to settle the dispute over slavery by dividing the lands acquired through the Louisiana

Purchase at the latitude of 36° 30². Slavery would be permitted in territories south of that latitude and, with the exception of Missouri, it would be banned in territories to the north. But this resolution, known as the Missouri Compromise, only postponed the growing crisis.

As the rich western territories applied to Congress for admission to the Union, the debate over slavery intensified. When, in 1849, California applied for admission as a free state, the dispute rose to a frenzied height that threatened to split the country in half. The South saw the admission of California as the first step toward overthrowing slavery everywhere; the balance of power between North and South would be destroyed. South Carolina announced that it was ready to secede from the Union if California were admitted. In the North, fanatic abolitionists also argued for secession. Since 1843, William Lloyd Garrison's abolitionist newspaper, the *Liberator,* had carried the provocative slogan "No Union with Slaveholders" on its masthead. But Congress was determined to hold the young, sprawling Union together. The people of California had, of their own free will, chosen to join the Union as a free state, and they would not be denied.

To placate angry southerners, a compromise was proposed. California would be admitted as a free state; the territories of Utah and New Mexico would be organized without restrictions on slavery; and, as a concession to the South, a stringent new law would be enacted to deal with the increasing numbers of fugitive slaves who were escaping to the North, and to punish those who helped them.

While the debates that were to have such a profound impact on the future of the nation were raging in Congress, the Stowes were engaged in planning their own future. Calvin looked forward eagerly to earning a larger salary as professor of Natural and Revealed Religion at Bowdoin, the college from which he had graduated and where he had spent some of the happiest years of his life. Although Hatty knew that even with the promise of a larger income, hard times still lay ahead for her and her family, she was elated by the prospect

of moving back to New England, her "real" home. Her brothers were already in the East and Lyman Beecher, who was
now seventy-five years old, planned to leave the management of Lane Seminary to others and to move east himself
within the year. It would be wonderful to have her family
close by. Even the knowledge that she was pregnant again
did nothing to diminish her high spirits.

When the time came to leave, a replacement had not
yet been found for Calvin, and he felt obliged to remain in
Cincinnati until someone could be found to take his place at
Lane. It was decided that Hatty, together with three of the
children, would journey ahead to Maine while she was still
able to travel. Calvin and the other two children would follow later.

In April 1850, the Stowes gathered at the Cincinnati
boat landing to say good-bye to one another. Dressed in
worn, shabby clothes and surrounded by children and bag-
gage, Hatty looked small and rather pathetic. She was almost
thirty-nine years old and six months pregnant, but her large
eyes shone with happiness and her heart was filled with joy.

It was an arduous journey for Hatty, traveling by boat,
stagecoach, and train, and struggling with bags and children
through jostling crowds. In her purse, she carried only a
small amount of money, which she doled out carefully for
the cheapest tickets and the barest necessities. She was tired
and weary, but the further east she traveled the happier she
became.

On arrival in New York, she stopped to visit her brother,
the Reverend Henry Ward Beecher, who, as the pastor of the
Plymouth Church in Brooklyn, was fast becoming one of the
most famous preachers in the nation. It was immediately
obvious to Hatty that her brother's flamboyant oratory was
well rewarded. He was earning the handsome salary of $3,300
per year; he lived rent free in a comfortable, well-furnished
house; and his wealthy congregation had just made him the
gift of a fine horse and carriage.

Although Hatty was awed by Henry Ward's financial

success, she was even more impressed by the nightly conversations around her brother's dinner table where every evening Henry Ward played host to friends and acquaintances. The talk centered mainly on the Fugitive Slave Act, part of the proposed legislation, called the Compromise of 1850, that was being debated in Congress.

In the past, northern states had been required to deliver escaped slaves to the South, but many northern states had passed laws giving fugitives the rights of habeas corpus and trial by jury, and imposing criminal penalties on kidnappers. It was up to federal agents to return escaped slaves to their owners, but no slave could be returned without a court hearing. Some states refused to cooperate in any way with federal agents engaged in hunting down fugitives.

But all of this would change when the Fugitive Slave Act became law. Federal agents would be empowered to track down slaves who had fled to the North, capture them, and return them to their owners. The agents would have absolute control of the captured slaves, and stiff criminal penalties would await anyone who harbored fugitives or otherwise obstructed their capture. If a federal agent refused to help a slave owner recapture his property, he would be fined one thousand dollars. On the other hand, an agent would receive a bonus of ten dollars for each fugitive he delivered. Generous fees would also be paid to federal commissioners who approved slaveholders' claims of ownership of escaped blacks. The expenses of capturing and returning slaves were to be paid by the federal government.

The situation was ripe for unprecedented injustice and massive corruption. The power of the law rested totally on the side of the slaveholders. All black people, even those who were free and had the documents to prove their freedom, were at the mercy of the slave catchers. Once they were seized, they no longer had the right to have their cases heard in a court of law. Pity the poor black person who fell into the hands of an unscrupulous federal agent.

Seated in the family pew, Hatty listened with pride as

Henry Ward Beecher denounced the proposed legislation from the pulpit of his Brooklyn church. He had become a staunch, uncompromising abolitionist, and his speech was plain and bold. When Henry Ward proclaimed that men and women who were true Christians would be morally compelled to break the Fugitive Slave Law, Hatty passionately agreed. It was a hateful, iniquitous law, one that would not only give the southern slaveholder the right to seize any black whom he claimed as a slave but that would command northern citizens to assist in the revolting business. It seemed to Hatty as though the entire country would soon experience at first hand the same kind of scenes she had witnessed in Cincinnati, that slavery would extend all over the North and overgrow the institutions of free society.

Hatty found it hard to tear herself away from further conversations with her brother, but time was pressing and she had to resume her journey. Her next stop was Hartford for an affectionate reunion with her sisters, Mary and Isabella, and her friend, Georgiana. Then, it was on to Boston where she and the children spent a week with her brother, the Reverend Edward Beecher, and his family. At the time, Edward was the pastor of the famous Park Street Church in Boston. Like Henry Ward, Edward and his wife, Isabella, were ardent abolitionists. Ever since his friend, Dr. Lovejoy, was murdered, Edward Beecher had been a fierce opponent of slavery.

Again in Edward's home, Hatty found herself drawn into conversations about the impending Fugitive Slave Law. By the time she reached Brunswick, Maine, a few weeks later, her mind was on fire with indignation at the new wrongs about to be inflicted on the defenseless and innocent. She wanted to strike out against slavery. Christian morality, as well as her own deep compassion, demanded that she do so. But Hatty still did not know what she herself could do that would make a difference.

A blustery, northeast storm was raging along the Maine coast when Hatty and the children arrived in Brunswick on

Harriet Beecher Stowe's birthplace
in Litchfield, Connecticut

Lyman Beecher, the most influential
clergyman of his time, exerted a lasting
influence on the lives of his children.

Catherine Beecher, Harriet's older
sister, was famous for her
pioneering work in education.

(Above) An 1838 view of the waterfront at
Cincinnati, Ohio, showing the Ohio River and
the shores of slaveholding Kentucky beyond

(Facing page) The front page of the
September 2, 1839, issue of the *Emancipator,*
an antislavery newspaper, depicting abuses
and cruelties suffered by slaves

EMANCIPATOR—*EXTRA*.

NEW-YORK, SEPTEMBER 2, 1839.

American Anti-Slavery Almanac for 1840.

The seven cuts following, are selected from thirteen, which may be found in the Anti-Slavery Almanac for 1840. They represent well-authenticated facts, and illustrate in various ways, the cruelties daily inflicted upon three millions of native born Americans, by their fellow-countrymen! A brief explanation follows each cut.

The peculiar "Domestic Institutions of our Southern brethren."

Selling a Mother from her Child.

Mothers with young Children at work in the field.

A Woman chained to a Girl, and a Man in irons at work in the field.

"They can't take care of themselves"; explained in an interesting article.

Hunting Slaves with dogs and guns. A Slave drowned by the dogs.

Servility of the Northern States in arresting and returning fugitive Slaves.

(Above) Slaves were sold like cattle, and their families were torn apart during auctions such as this. Slaves could expect to be sold at least once during their lives.

(Below) A station on the Underground Railroad, the secret network that helped slaves escape and hid them from slave hunters

Harriet Beecher Stowe in 1850, shortly
before she began writing *Uncle Tom's Cabin*

(Above) Amid the protests of onlookers, two runaway slaves are marched through the streets of Boston before their return to slavery by soldiers acting under authority of the Fugitive Slave Law.

(Right) An instant best-seller, Stowe's novel sold out wherever it appeared. Four separate editions are offered in this early advertisement.

Mrs. Stowe and her husband, Professor
Calvin Stowe, surrounded by characters from
her famous novel. Clockwise from top left:
Simon Legree; Topsy; Eliza fleeing across
the ice; Uncle Tom and Little Eva.

(Above) In 1855, the illustrious Beechers gathered
to celebrate the completion of their father's
autobiography. Standing, left to right, are:
Thomas, William, Edward, Charles, Henry Ward.
Seated, left to right, are: Isabella, Catherine,
Dr. Lyman Beecher, Mary, Harriet.

(Facing page) Passions roused during
abolitionist meetings sometimes erupted into
violence. Here, an 1858 meeting in Boston's
Tremont Temple is being broken up.

(Above) Lyman Beecher with his two most
famous children, Harriet and Henry Ward.
This rare photo was taken in 1861, the
year in which the Civil War began.

(Facing page) Currier and Ives, the
popular lithographers, issued this idealized
portrait of Lincoln to commemorate
the Emancipation Proclamation.

May 22, 1850. They were all wet and shivering with cold. To make matters worse, the storm delayed the arrival of their luggage and household goods. Once again, Hatty had to put aside her thoughts in order to deal with more immediate problems.

First, there was the big, old yellow house on Federal Street, which the Stowes had rented sight unseen. It had stood vacant for several years, was damp and musty, and smelled of mold and mildew. Undaunted, Hatty immediately set to work to make it liveable. Despite the fact that she was in the final weeks of her pregnancy, she spent the month of June in a frantic spree of cleaning, painting walls, varnishing floors, laying carpets, building chairs out of old barrels, nailing up shelves, sewing bed linens, and installing the few pieces of furniture that had finally arrived from Boston. The house lacked a sink, the water pump needed fixing, and new cisterns to catch rainwater had to be installed, so Hatty was forced to spend some of her fast-dwindling funds to hire a man to do the work.

Despite all the problems, Hatty's spirit never faltered as she saw to everything. But even her stoic patience had its limits. When Calvin sent her long, gloomy letters, complaining that he was out of money, that his health was poor, and that he doubted that he would live long enough to see her again, Hatty, in an uncharacteristic outburst of anger, tore them up and threw them into the fire. Then, thinking better of her action, she sat down and wrote to Calvin, "You are not able just now to bear anything, my dear husband, therefore trust all to me; I never doubt or despair." Knowing that the stability and security of the family rested in her hands, Hatty brushed aside her own concerns to make plans for the future. She told Calvin that she was already "making arrangements with editors to raise money."[3]

By the time Calvin arrived in July with the two remaining children, the house was ready. One week later, on July 8, 1850, Hatty gave birth to her seventh and last child. The baby was named Charles Edward in memory of the baby,

Samuel Charles, who had died in Cincinnati. Years later, Charles Edward Stowe would make his own claim to fame by writing his mother's biography.

The summer passed pleasantly enough, with picnics and berry-picking parties that the children enjoyed, but the brief vacation was all too short. As autumn approached, the Stowes came face to face with some hard realities. The arrival of Calvin's successor at Lane had been delayed and Calvin was asked to return to Cincinnati to teach for another year. Although he had no desire to spend another year at Lane, he felt a strong obligation to do so. The trustees at Bowdoin were sympathetic to Calvin's plight, and allowed him to postpone his commitment to join their faculty.

The consequences of this decision threatened to be disastrous for the Stowe family. While Calvin returned to Lane, Hatty would have to remain with the six children in Maine. Even under the best of circumstances, it would be hard for Hatty to manage the children and the household by herself. But the fact was that the family's expenses for the year would amount to three hundred dollars more than Calvin would earn. Unless Hatty sold more of her writings, the family faced extreme hardships and certain bankruptcy.

Once again, Hatty found herself in the center of a domestic maelstrom. Describing her hectic life in a letter to Edward's wife, Isabella, she wrote,

Since I began this note I have been called off at least a dozen times; once for the fish-man, to buy a codfish; once to see a man who had brought me some barrels of apples; once to see a book-man; then to Mrs. Upham, to see about a drawing I promised to make for her; then to nurse the baby; then into the kitchen to make a chowder for dinner; and now I am at it again, for nothing but deadly determination enables me ever to write; it is rowing against wind and tide.[4]

Nevertheless, Hatty rowed with all her strength and steered a true course through the storm. She cleared a space on the kitchen table and set to work in earnest, churning out piece after piece. She sent some of her articles to the *National Era,* a new weekly that upheld strong antislavery principles but also published "original sketches and tales for home reading."

Unlike William Lloyd Garrison's radical *Liberator,* the *National Era,* which counted John Greenleaf Whittier and Nathaniel Hawthorne among it contributors, hoped to rouse the moral conscience of its readers and "appeal to the southern people as men of like passions with ourselves." Hatty, most of whose articles and stories dealt with moral and domestic issues, was the kind of writer that the editor, Gamaliel Bailey, hoped to encourage. Between August 1850 and January 1851, Hatty sold four pieces to the *National Era,* including a mild satire about an impractical scholar (based on Calvin's attempts to grow a garden); an article on Christmas; a story denouncing late parties; and a tale entitled "The Freeman's Dream: A Parable," an antislavery story in which she advanced the view that the laws of God were above "an act of Congress, or an interpretation of the United States Constitution." With this story, Hatty took a tentative step toward entering the debate over slavery. Still, she felt, it was not enough, she yearned to do more.

In late September 1850, dreadful news reached Maine. Hoping to forestall a bloody conflict, Congress had acted and on September 20, President Millard Fillmore had signed the Fugitive Slave Act into law. Northerners who until then had paid little attention to the slavery question were roused from their indifference by the heartrending scenes that they soon witnessed around them. The capture of fugitive slaves began in earnest.

In the weeks that followed, Hatty received letter after letter from Edward's wife, Isabella, describing events in Boston. Anxious to protect their investments in the South, many wealthy Bostonians proclaimed their intention of upholding the law. The streets of Boston, the "cradle of liberty," were opened to the slave hunters.

Black people were not safe anywhere, not even in their homes. Slave hunters broke down their doors in the dead of night and dragged them away. Blacks were arrested suddenly on the streets and at their jobs. Black families who had lived in Boston for many years were torn apart. A wave of panic swept through northern black communities. Some blacks stowed away on ships bound for Europe, while others quickly gathered whatever they could carry and fled further north. During the last three months of 1850, more than three thousand blacks sought refuge in Canada, and many more were to follow in the years to come.

With a growing sense of righteous anger, Hatty read newspaper reports about the increasing incidents of violence and injustice. In New York City, a free black man was kidnapped and shipped South on the claim that he was owned by a man in Baltimore. A respected black tailor who had prospered for many years in Poughkeepsie, New York, was seized and sent to South Carolina. A Philadelphia woman was arrested on the word of a man who said she had escaped more than twenty years earlier; for good measure, the man also laid claim to the woman's six children who had been born in freedom. Men, women, and children whose desperate courage had driven them to find freedom in the North were at the mercy of the slave catchers.

The situation in Boston became worse. Abolitionists announced their defiance of the law, declaring, "it is to be denounced, resisted, disobyed. . . . As moral and religious men, [we] cannot obey an immoral and irreligious statute."[5] When protesters tried to prevent the capture of William and Ellen Craft, a celebrated black couple who had made a dramatic escape from the South, President Fillmore threatened to send in federal troops. Theodore Parker, pastor of the church to which the Crafts belonged, helped them escape. He then sent a letter to Fillmore, saying, "I must reverence the laws of God, come of that what will come. . . . You cannot think that I am to stand by and see my own church carried off to slavery and do nothing."[6]

One day, Hatty received another letter from Edward Beecher's wife. Isabella Beecher had written an impassioned letter, full of outrage at the rising number of incidents, full of anger at the federal troops who were policing the streets of Boston, and, finally, full of despair at her own and Edward's inability to do anything that could make a difference. In a final note of frustration, Isabella wrote, "Hatty, if I could use a pen as you can, I would write something that will make this whole nation feel what an accursed thing slavery is."[7]

The children were gathered in the parlor when Hatty sat down in a chair to read the letter. The baby was napping in the cradle at her side. The older children were reading and working on their lessons, while the younger ones played and chattered around her feet. Suddenly, Hatty looked up and told the children to pay attention while she read them their aunt's letter. Years later, the twins, Harriet and Eliza, and their brothers Henry, Frederick, and Charles, recalled the tone of urgency in their mother's voice as she read the letter aloud. They remembered all their lives how their mother rose to her feet with the letter in her small hand, and how she looked at each of them in turn with eyes fired with determination. And they never forgot how their mother, in answer to Aunt Isabella's challenge, announced to them fervently, "I will write something. I will—if I live!"[8]

Winter comes early in Maine, and with it, that year, came deep snows and bitter cold. Strong winds rocked the old house and most of the rooms were freezing. Hatty and the children retreated into the warmest ones, but it was so cold that the children could barely sit through their meals, even though the table was set near a glowing stove. During the day, Hatty could not even think of writing; as soon as she tried to snatch a few moments for herself, one or another of the children demanded attention. In December, she wrote to Isabella, "As long as the baby sleeps with me nights I can't do much at anything, but I will do it at last. I will write that thing."[9]

She still had no idea what form "that thing" would take; she would think about it later. First, there were other, more urgent things that demanded to be written, articles and stories that she had already promised to the *National Era* and other publications. The family depended on the money she could earn by writing, and she would have to churn out those works before she could begin to think of writing anything else. But she could accomplish nothing during the daytime when every moment was filled with noisy interruptions. She would have to work at night, after the children were in bed.

As a fresh storm blanketed the world outside with snow, Hatty set up a table near the fireplace in the parlor to escape the icy drafts that whistled through the house. Seated there, with the cold winds howling outside, an old shawl draped over her shoulders, she worked on an article that was promised to a certain editor. But as she worked, strange thoughts filled her mind, thoughts that she could not push away. She swept the pages of the article to one side, spread a clean sheet of paper squarely in front of her, dipped her pen into the inkstand, and with an urgency she had never known before, she began to write.

CHAPTER 9

UNCLE TOM'S CABIN

THE YEAR was 1850, midpoint of the century. The nation was balanced precariously on the fulcrum of slavery, teetering between the principles of freedom and justice on one hand, and the destruction of liberty and democracy on the other. All over America, people were weighing the questions, wondering which way the scales would tip. Something was needed, some sign, some event, that would point the way to the future. No one imagined that the catalyst for change would come from the pen of a frail, overworked woman, the wife of an impoverished clergyman and mother of six.

Certainly, Hatty herself had no intimations of the future as she read over what she had written. She knew only that she was deeply dissatisfied. Always a rapid writer, she believed that time was money and should not be wasted in revising or correcting her work. That, she insisted, was what editors were for. But this "thing" was different. She was writing not just for "the pay," but to rouse people from their complacency, to shock their consciences, and to rattle their souls. She wanted to show northerners the real character of slavery, and demonstrate to southerners that the evils of slavery lay in the system itself rather than in the people involved in it. This "thing" failed to do that; it was too preachy, too abstract. She tore up the pages, vowing to start over. But how was she to do it? Night after night, after the children were put to bed, Hatty sat before the fire, staring into the flames, but her mind remained blank. This "thing" would not be as easy to write as she had first supposed.

Christmas arrived, bringing with it a fresh snowfall. Calvin Stowe was still in Cincinnati, so Hatty bought sleds for the children and joined in their play. They had noisy snowball fights, built snowmen, and tumbled down the hillside with raucous laughter. Perhaps it was an effect of the brisk, cold air and the bright winter sunshine, but whatever the cause, Hatty, despite her thirty-nine years, her "six children and cares endless," looked healthier and prettier than ever that winter. Crises and hard times had marked her features with character and determination, but her fine skin was still soft, her cheeks glowed, and her large eyes and full mouth smiled at the world with candid charm.

When January came, Hatty was still struggling for ideas. Then, late one night, during a raging blizzard, Henry Ward surprised his sister with a visit. After battling his way from the railway station, he appeared at Hatty's door, half frozen and covered with snow. She helped him inside and quickly piled more wood on the fire. All night long, brother and sister huddled near the glowing flames and talked.

For several years, Henry Ward had been preaching against slavery from the pulpit and writing articles for an abolitionist paper. Now, as she listened to her brother describe his bold new schemes for agitating against the "peculiar institution," Hatty found herself caught up in his passionate intensity and decided to tell him of her own plans to write about slavery.

Henry Ward greeted her revelation enthusiastically, but warned her that the challenge that lay ahead would be difficult, and possibly dangerous. Abolitionists, even in the enlightened climate of New England, were considered wild-eyed radicals. By publicly avowing her views about slavery, Hatty would join the ranks of that "small, despised, unfashionable band." Derision and insults would certainly be heaped on her. She and her family might even become the targets of violence. And, by daring to speak out on a serious political issue, she would risk condemnation by people who believed that women writers should restrict their scribbling to domestic topics "appropriate" to women. Nevertheless, before Henry Ward left the following morning, he urged her to, "Do it, Hatty, do it!"[1]

Her brother's whirlwind visit left Hatty filled with new determination. Henry Ward had encouraged her to paint vivid pictures for her readers, pictures that would show them the grim realities of slavery and make them feel the agonies of slavery in a way that no preaching or explaining could ever do. But how should she begin? Which of the many horrors she knew about should she describe? Weeks passed, and still Hatty had no answers.

Then, one Sunday morning in February, while sitting in church with her family, a strange thing happened. As the minister droned on, Hatty fell into one of her abstracted moods. Suddenly, a scene flashed into her mind as clearly and intensely as though it were being played out in front of her eyes. She saw two black men with hate-filled, brutal faces savagely beating an old man as black as themselves. A sneering white man stood by, urging them on, while demanding that the old man confess to something. What was it the master wanted from the old slave? Never mind. Whatever it was, the old man refused. As each blow of the lash cut cruelly into his quivering flesh, he looked with pity at his tormentors. Finally, with his dying breath, he whispered his forgiveness of them. Who was this Christ-like black man? Hatty did not know, but she knew that he was important to her. The scene, so vivid and real, had "blown into her mind as by the rushing of a mighty wind."[2]

Still in a trance, she walked home, sat down at the desk, and began to write down the vision she had seen. After a while, she laid down her pen, summoned the children to the sitting room, and, in a voice trembling with emotion, read aloud what she had written. Tears filled her children's eyes, and one of the younger ones sobbed, "Oh Mama! Slavery is the most cruel thing in the world."[3] As she looked at the solemn faces of her children, Hatty knew that she had written something very powerful.

The sketch told how Uncle Tom (the old man's name had come to her as clearly as the other details in her vision) escaped from bondage, but it did not tell about slavery itself. Why had Uncle Tom's master ordered him whipped to death? What events led him to this violent, bloody end? Hatty did not know. She put the sketch away, hoping that somehow the story would reveal itself to her. In the weeks that followed, she "owled about," performing her daily chores almost unconsciously, while her mind filled with memories of all the black people she had known and all the scenes of slavery she had witnessed back in Cincinnati.

Calvin returned home in March, and the household bustled with renewed activity. One day, while searching for some papers, he discovered Hatty's sketch. Deeply moved by what he read, Calvin found his wife in the kitchen and, in a tear-filled voice, said, "Hatty, this is the climax of that story . . . begin at the beginning and work up to this and you'll have your book."[4]

Suddenly, Hatty knew how her story would develop. She glimpsed the opening scene, and could vaguely discern the currents of a plot that would sweep Uncle Tom along to his inevitable, tragic end. She would write it in installments for publication in a magazine, with each section being a story almost complete in itself, much the way Charles Dickens and other well-known authors of the time wrote their books.

Hatty set to work immediately. Still unaware of how far the story would lead her, she wrote to Dr. Gamaliel Bailey, editor of the *National Era,* enclosing the first installment and offering the project to him for publication. The story, she explained,

will be a much longer one than any I have ever
written, embracing a series of sketches which
give the lights and shadows of the "patriarchal
institution". . . . I feel now that the time is come
when even a woman or a child who can speak a
word for freedom and humanity is bound to
speak. . . . My vocation is simply that of painter,
and my object will be to hold up [slavery] in the
most lifelike and graphic manner possible. . . .
There is no arguing with pictures, *and every-*
body is impressed by them, whether they mean
to be or not. . . . The thing may extend through
three or four numbers. It will be ready in two or
three weeks.[5]

Hatty was pleased by Dr. Bailey's prompt acceptance and by his handsome offer of three hundred dollars for the story that was to run in "three or four" issues of the magazine.

The first installment appeared in the May 1851 issue of the *National Era* under the title "Uncle Tom's Cabin; or, the Man That Was a Thing." (Later, Hatty would change the title to "Uncle Tom's Cabin or, Life Among the Lowly.") By the time the fourth installment was written, Hatty realized that the story would be much longer than she had originally intended. But there was no stopping now; characters leapt into her mind, and scene after scene appeared to her with vivid reality, demanding to be written.

Still, Hatty realized that if her story was to accomplish its purpose, she would need to draw on more than her own imagination, memories, and experiences. She needed facts. She immersed herself in books, newspapers, magazines, sermons, accounts by former slaves—indeed, everything about slavery that she could lay her hands on. To learn more about the innermost thoughts and feelings of slaves, as well as details of plantation life "from one who has been an actual laborer on one,"[6] she wrote to Frederick Douglass, the former slave who had become famous as an abolitionist orator and editor. Thus begun, their correspondence ripened into a lifelong friendship.

She read *Slavery As It Is* by Theodore Weld, the young man whose abolitionist activities had caused Lyman Beecher so much trouble at Lane Seminary. And she analyzed the laws governing slavery in the various southern states. Hatty was particularly horrified by the laws outlined in the notorious *Code Noir* (Black Code) of Louisiana, and she kept a copy of it close at hand throughout the writing of her book.

When a spring thaw made the roads to Boston passable, Hatty paid a visit to the Edward Beechers, who were delighted to give her all the help they could. Edward lent her his considerable collection of books on slavery, obtained others from fellow abolitionists, and introduced her to several former slaves whose stories she later incorporated in her book.

Day after day, Hatty worked at fever pitch, snatching the time to write when and where she could. When she ran out of writing paper, she used the brown paper in which groceries were wrapped. The children, being children, interrupted her constantly. Whenever Calvin needed the desk for his own purposes, Hatty moved her papers to the kitchen table. Then summer came, and Lyman Beecher descended on the household for a month-long stay. He was getting old and a little forgetful, but he was full of great plans for editing all of his sermons prior to publishing them in one immense book. He commandeered the desk and spread his papers all over the house, so Hatty, who loved her father dearly, retreated to the back steps without complaint and continued to write.

The book was far from complete. Dr. Bailey became uneasy. He worried that readers would grow tired of the long story, but when a storm of letters poured in to the magazine begging Mrs. Stowe "not to hurry through Uncle Tom,"[7] he urged her to keep on.

Hatty pressed on at a furious pace, but more distractions came when sister Catherine, who had become a somewhat self-righteous spinster, published a tract condemning the women's suffrage movement on the grounds that a woman's place was in the home, nursery, and school. Henry Ward, who supported the women's crusade for the vote, told Lyman Beecher that he thought Catherine was mentally unstable. A furor erupted, and Hatty was called upon to act as peacemaker between the volatile members of her family.

Despite the turmoil around her, Hatty continued to write feverishly. It was as though the tale had taken on a life of its own, demanding to be told. The story that was to run in "three or four numbers" of the *National Era* eventually grew to forty installments in length. As each new installment was published, the fame of Hatty's story spread. Week after week, the magazine was sold out. Copies were worn out as readers passed them from hand to hand; then they were carefully saved "as if the tear stains on them were sacred."

It was a powerful novel, filled with memorable characters and incidents drawn from life, and, unlike any novel before, its hero, Uncle Tom, was a black man—a courageous slave, moreover, whose dignity and strength grew not out of resignation but from a profound Christian faith. The story opens with Uncle Tom living with his wife and children in a tidy little cabin on a Kentucky plantation owned by Mr. Shelby, a good-natured, kindly, but improvident man. Another slave, Eliza, and her little son Harry are also owned by Mr. Shelby, but Eliza's husband, George, belongs to the cruel Mr. Harris, a neighboring planter. Unable to endure Harris's brutality, George decides to escape, planning to buy freedom for his wife and child when he reaches Canada.

After George leaves, Eliza learns that circumstances have forced Mr. Shelby to sell Uncle Tom and her son Harry to a slave trader. That night, after warning Uncle Tom of the impending disaster, Eliza wraps Harry in her arms and flees. While Eliza journeys north, Haley, the slave trader, takes Uncle Tom on a steamboat down the Mississippi River. Among the passengers are a five-year-old white girl named

Eva and her father, Augustine St. Clare, a wealthy New Orleans plantation owner. When Eva accidentally falls over-
board, Tom jumps in to save her. In gratitude, St. Clare buys
Tom from Haley. Although he misses his family, Tom is
happy enough on St. Clare's plantation until Eva falls ill and
dies, and St. Clare, crushed by the loss of his beloved daughter, dies soon after.

Meanwhile, after their dramatic escapes, George, Eliza,
and Harry have reunited and found freedom in Canada. Then
once again Tom is sold, this time to a former New Englander,
an evil, depraved man named Simon Legree. Poor Tom suf-
fers terrible abuses on Legree's Louisiana plantation, but
nothing can shatter his spirit or break his unwavering faith.
When Cassy, a beautiful mulatto slave who had been forced
to be Legree's mistress, decides to escape, Tom refuses to
betray her, even on the point of death. As he is being beaten,
Tom has only words of forgiveness for his tormenters. Tom
dies shortly before the arrival of George Shelby, son of his
old Kentucky master, who has come to buy him back. When
Shelby learns what has happened to Tom, he returns to
Kentucky, frees all his slaves, and vows to dedicate himself
to the cause of abolition.

It was all there, everything Hatty knew and thought and
felt about slavery. In Uncle Tom, who faithfully followed the
principles of loving others and forgiving those who did him
harm, she had created a Christ-like hero who would stir the
emotions of the readers of her day. By contrasting Tom's
moral purity and virtue with the cruelty of the system that
kept him in bondage, she forced her readers to confront the
depravity and injustice of slavery. And to those who believed
that slaves were inferior and less than human, she offered
another kind of hero in the character of George Harris. When
George and Eliza are surrounded by slave hunters, George
proclaims,

I am George Harris. A Mr. Harris, of Kentucky,
did call me his property. But now I'm a free

man, standing on God's free soil; and my wife
and my child I claim as mine. . . . We have arms
to defend ourselves and we mean to do it. You
want to send [us] back to be whipped and tor-
tured, and ground down under the heels of them
that you call masters; and your laws will bear
you out in it. . . . But you haven't got us. We
don't own your laws; we don't own your country;
we stand here as free, under God's sky, as you
are; and, by the great God that made us, we'll
fight for our liberty or die.[8]

With George's "declaration of independence," Hatty made the daring pronouncement that courage and heroism were not the exclusive province of whites.

Hatty had tried to show that many slaveholders, like the Shelbys and St. Clare, were civilized and kind, but that they, like the slaves themselves, were victims of the "peculiar institution." It was not them, but the cruelties of slavery that she had sought to expose. She had argued that, in a truly Christian world, slavery could not exist: that its perpetuation was partly the fault of the churches which, instead of practicing religion, had engaged in hairsplitting arguments that allowed the evils and wickedness of slavery to flourish. She had shown that northerners were equally to blame, that they had no reason to feel morally superior as long as they supported the Compromise of 1850 and the Fugitive Slave Law, and as long as northern factories profited from materials supplied by slave labor. Because she had tried to present a balanced picture, Hatty was afraid that the more radical abolitionists would be disappointed. But she hoped her arguments would arouse the moral indigantion of thoughtful people from all sections of the country. If they banded together, slavery could be destroyed peacefully, without bloodshed, in a manner that would be least harmful to everyone.

After a year of unremitting toil, the book was finished. It was March 1852. As she laid down her pen, Hatty felt a tremendous sense of release. Years later, she wrote that "the indignation, the pity, the distress, that had long weighed upon [my] soul seemed to pass off,"[9] as she finished *Uncle Tom's Cabin.* In some mysterious way, as she wrote about the escapes of slaves, she had managed to loose herself from bondage as well. She stepped outdoors, and as the crisp New England wind whipped through her hair, she experienced a sense of happiness and freedom she had never known before.

Meanwhile, the serialized "Uncle Tom's Cabin" was creating such a stir that it came to the attention of John P. Jewett, a Boston book publisher who owned a new, power-operated printing press. He offered Hatty 50 percent of the profits if she would share the expenses of printing "Uncle Tom's Cabin" in book form. If those terms were unacceptable, he would give her a straight 10-percent royalty on sales of the book.

It was clear to Calvin and Hatty that they could not afford to pay half of the production costs of the book. The Stowes simply had no money. While she was writing *Uncle Tom's Cabin,* Hatty had not been able to produce other financially rewarding work. Her total income for the year was the three hundred dollars she had received from the *National Era* for writing a story "three or four" numbers in length. Hatty would have to settle for a simple royalty. Calvin went to Boston to meet with Jewett, and on March 13, 1852, the contract was signed.

Although the last installment of the story would not appear in the *National Era* until April, Mr. Jewett's press began to roll. One week later, on March 20, five thousand copies of *Uncle Tom's Cabin,* published as a two-volume set priced at $1.50, went on sale. Calvin returned from Boston, bringing with him the first copies. It was very satisfying to hold the thick, neatly bound volumes in her hand. Hatty calculated that if, by some miracle, all five thousand copies sold, she would earn $750. She might be able to buy a new silk dress—but that seemed almost too much to hope for.

No one, least of all Hatty, was prepared for what happened next. Within two days, all five thousand copies of the first edition were sold. A second edition appeared the following week, and a third edition was published on April 1, the same day on which the final installment of the book appeared in the *National Era*. Three steam presses and an army of bookbinders worked day and night to meet the continuing demand. By the end of the year, 300 thousand copies of the book had been sold in the United States. In Great Britain, where Hatty had no copyright and therefore received no royalties, more than 1.5 million copies were in circulation. Translators were already hard at work and, within two years, the book would be available in thirty-seven languages around the world.

Four months after the first books rolled off the presses, Hatty received a royalty payment of ten thousand dollars. It was a fortune in those days—more money than she and Calvin had ever imagined—and it was only the first of many payments she would receive in the years to come. The long, weary struggle with poverty was over. And Hatty would have her new silk dress.

In a few short weeks, *Uncle Tom's Cabin* and its unknown author had taken the world by storm.

CHAPTER 10

IN THE EYE
OF A STORM

IN REPLYING to a letter from a woman who asked that she describe herself, Hatty wrote, "To begin, then, I am a little bit of a woman, somewhat more than forty, about as thin and dry as a pinch of snuff; never very much to look at in my best days, and looking like a used-up article now."[1] Her modest description was meant not so much for the correspondent, but to assure herself that she was still the same old Hatty.

Indeed, Hatty and Calvin Stowe could hardly believe what was happening; everything seemed unreal. But every day torrents of letters flooded in, confirming the fact that *Uncle Tom's Cabin* was touching the hearts and minds of men and women everywhere. The poet John Greenleaf Whittier offered "Ten thousand thanks for thy immortal book."[2] Henry Wadsworth Longfellow sent a letter saying, "It is one of the greatest triumphs recorded in literary history, to say nothing of the higher triumph of its moral effect."[3] And the great English novelist Charles Dickens wrote, "I have read your book with the deepest interest and sympathy, and admire, more than I can express to you, both the generous feeling which inspired it, and the admirable power with which it is executed."[4]

In April, the *Independent,* an influential religious paper, proclaimed, "Let *all men* read it!"[5] Then came a letter from the editors asking if Hatty would travel to New York to discuss writing for the paper. A trip would be a welcome diversion, and she could use the occasion for stopovers to visit with family and friends.

As she said good-bye to Calvin and the children at the Brunswick station, she was still the careworn housewife and anxious, loving mother who had become a "literary lady" through necessity. But her eyes shone with excitement. What a luxury this small vacation would be! As Hatty climbed into the railway car, she had no idea that she was stepping into a different world—a world that would never again allow her to be just plain Hatty.

She stopped first in Boston to visit Edward and his wife, and was amazed to find that everyone was talking about the book. She wrote to Calvin that she was "in such a whirl" and that Mr. Jewett was working day and night to keep up with the public's demand. She saw her father, too, and was pleased to have Lyman Beecher's congratulations. The final volume of his sermons was about to be published, and when he jokingly observed that her book might outsell his, Hatty laughed. Then it was on to Hartford and New Haven for visits with her sister Mary and her friends, Georgiana May Sykes and Mary Dutton. Everyone showered Hatty with praise and congratulations.

Not until she arrived at Henry Ward's home in New York, however, did Hatty begin to realize the immensity of what was happening. As one of the nation's most famous preachers, Henry Ward Beecher was in constant demand by religious groups, women's suffrage assemblies, and antislavery societies. So when Hatty accompanied her brother to these gatherings, she was amazed to discover that it was she, not her brother, who was the center of attention. A whisper that Mrs. Stowe was present was enough to disrupt a meeting and send a rush of admirers to crowd around her. And when Hatty casually remarked that she was sorry that tickets to a concert by Jenny Lind were sold out, two free

tickets appeared almost miraculously, sent by the world famous "Swedish Nightingale" herself. The concert, she told
Calvin, was "a bewildering dream of sweetness and beauty."[6]

Indeed, Hatty's life itself had become a bewildering
dream in which all things seemed possible. Catherine was in
New York soliciting funds for a new school for girls, and
Hatty had the strange pleasure of giving her sister a donation
and allowing her name to be listed as one of the school's
sponsors.

Even more rewarding was the opportunity to redeem
some slaves, just as Henry Ward had been doing for some
time. Four years before, Henry Ward had raised money to
purchase the freedom of two slave girls named Edmondson.
Since then, Hatty had contributed what she could to help
educate the girls. Now, the old slave mother of the girls
appeared on Henry Ward's doorstep to ask if his parishioners would redeem her two sons still held in slavery. Feeling
"a sacred call to be the helper of the helpless,"[7] Hatty inter-
vened. When the old woman finished her story, Hatty told
her, "Set your heart at rest; you and your children shall be
redeemed. If I can't raise the money otherwise, I will pay it
myself."[8] Before leaving New York, Hatty fulfilled her promise to raise the necessary funds; Milly Edmondson and her
children were set free. Uncomfortable with her sudden fame,
Hatty nevertheless had found a way to put it to good use.
Yet, she wrote to Calvin, "It is not fame nor praise that
contents me. I seem never to have needed love so much as
now. I long to hear you say how much you love me."[9]

Six weeks after leaving Brunswick, Hatty returned home
to hear that Calvin had good news of his own. He had been
offered the post of Professor of Sacred Literature at the Theological Seminary at Andover, Massachusetts, at twice the
salary he was paid at Bowdoin. The summer was spent moving to Andover and setting up house in an old stone coffin
factory that was renovated for their use. It was a charming,
comfortable home, and there they would live happily for the
next twelve years. After years of adversity, fortune was smiling on the Stowes.

Freed at last from endless drudgery—she had hired a cook, a housekeeper, and a governess to tend the children— Hatty turned her attention to answering the flood of letters that continued to pour in. At first, they were full of praise, but as the weeks wore on, she received an increasing number that were hateful, sometimes threatening and obscene; many of them were anonymous.

A public debate about *Uncle Tom's Cabin* had begun to rage in papers across the country between people—both northerners and southerners—whose compassion and human sympathy had been aroused, and those who denounced the book as a pack of lies. The *Atlanta Planter* attacked the "wicked authoress"[10] and her book, claiming that it was filled with falsehoods. The *New Orleans Crescent* also lashed out at Hatty, declaring, "There never before was anything so detestable or so monstrous among women as this," and the *Southern Literary Messenger* called her a "vile wretch in petticoats."[11] The New York *Journal of Commerce,* which represented the interests of bankers, manufacturers, cotton brokers, and others who had a great deal of money invested in the South or who did business with the southern market, published a scathing attack on *Uncle Tom's Cabin,* declaring it completely untrue. Even children were affected by the controversy. In Richmond, youngsters were chanting a new sidewalk song:

> *Go, go, go,*
> *Ol' Harriet Beecher Stowe!*
> *We don't want you here in Virginny—*
> *Go, go, go!*

Despite efforts to ban it, the book continued to sell so fast in the South and elsewhere that booksellers could not keep up with the demand. Meanwhile, a spate of "anti-Tom" literature began to appear in magazines and bookstores. At least fifteen books with such titles as *Aunt Phillis' Cabin, or Southern Life As It Is* and *Uncle Robin in His Cabin in Virginia and Tom Without One in Boston* were published by proslavery writers who attempted to show that blacks were a hopelessly inferior people who were better off under the protection of the slavery system, that relations between slaves and masters were friendly and even loving, that slavery was condoned by the Bible, and that slaves were happier and far more secure than free workers in northern factories. Just as the antislavery furor created by *Uncle Tom's Cabin* provoked southern anger, the "anti-Tom" literature was now spreading abolitionist feeling like wildfire through the North.

Then one day, upon opening a package addressed to Hatty, Calvin found an ear severed from the head of a slave. It was all too much for Hatty. She had told the truth about slavery in *Uncle Tom's Cabin,* and she was determined to prove it once and for all. She set to work immediately gathering a mountain of material to defend and document every detail in her book.

After several months of grueling labor, she finished *A Key to Uncle Tom's Cabin,* a compilation of case histories, letters, articles, handbills, trial transcripts, laws and legal documents, and slave testimonies, that not only verified what she had written in her novel but demonstrated in detail even greater brutalities and crueler conditions. What distinguished slavery from free servitude, she wrote, was "evil, and only evil." *A Key to Uncle Tom's Cabin* was written "with no pleasure, and with much pain," she said, but her object was "to bring the subject of slavery, as a moral and religious question, before the minds of those who profess to be followers of Christ."[12] She argued that the slave system made people callous and that countless cruelties were performed because slave owners were so inured to the system that they no longer regarded these acts as cruel. She also argued that the churches of America had failed in their moral obligation to society and that if they took a firm stand against slavery, it would be destroyed overnight. All men were equal in the eyes of God, she wrote, and any clergyman who refused to denounce slavery was actively supporting it.

Hatty finished writing *A Key to Uncle Tom's Cabin* in

February 1853. Three months later, the book was published by Mr. Jewett and, within a short time, more than 100,000 copies were sold. It seemed, however, that only Hatty's fans were interested. Although she had written the book to answer her critics, few copies were bought in the South.

In the meantime, Hatty received an exciting letter from the Glasgow Anti-Slavery Society inviting her to make a speaking tour of Scotland and England, and offering to pay all of her expenses, as well as those of Professor Stowe. Sixteen years before, when Calvin had taken his European trip, Hatty wished that she could go, too. Now, because of her own efforts, she was being offered a tour of the British Isles, all expenses paid! She dashed off a letter of acceptance.

After sending the children to stay with members of the Beecher clan, Hatty and Calvin set sail for England on March 30, 1853, accompanied by Hatty's brother, the Reverend Charles Beecher. Calvin would spend six weeks on the tour and then return home, while Hatty, with Charles as her escort, would continue on to Europe. Eleven days later, they arrived at Liverpool where they were greeted by a huge crowd. Everywhere they went, they were surrounded by adoring throngs eager for a word, a handclasp, or just a glimpse of the famous American writer. During a brief excursion through the English countryside, they were cheered by farmers, laborers, and children. Hatty and Calvin were nearly overwhelmed. "All that was anticipated by the newspapers, & ten times more, has befallen us," Calvin wrote in a letter home. "From the lowest peasant to the highest noble, wife is constantly beset, & I for her sake, so that we have not a moment's quiet."[13]

The Duke and Duchess of Sutherland invited Hatty, Calvin, and Charles to stay in their beautiful London residence. In what seemed to be an endless round of receptions, meetings, and dinners, Hatty met the great novelists Charles Dickens and William Makepeace Thackery, the Archbishop of Canterbury, political leaders Lord Palmerston and William

Gladstone, and a host of other prominent people. From London the three traveled by train to Scotland where their reception was even more dramatic. "Mrs. Beecher-Stowe" (as they called her in England) was everyone's idol. But Hatty, who went about in a modest straw bonnet and somber gray cape, often felt out of place. "I am always finding out, a day or two after, that I have been with somebody very remarkable, and did not know it at the time,"[14] she wrote in a letter home.

Since it was considered improper for a lady, even such a famous one as Hatty, to speak in public, it was Calvin who had to respond to welcome addresses and give one speech after another "in behalf of my wife." And it was Calvin who first noticed something disturbing as he sat at Hatty's side on platforms throughout Britain. Speech after speech that began as praise of Hatty soon turned into a diatribe against the United States, a terrible place where slavery was allowed to flourish. The British, it seemed, were finding that paying tribute to Mrs. Stowe gave them an opportunity to congratulate themselves for abolishing slavery in 1832 and to vent their anti-American feeling.

Calvin grew more disturbed by each new attack, but he held his tongue until, at a meeting in London in May, he rose to address a crowd of more than four thousand. Looking solemnly over the packed hall, he said that it was all very well for England to congratulate itself for freeing a few slaves in the outposts of her empire, but the situation in the United States was different. To suddenly abolish slavery would send the country and its three-billion-dollar economy into ruin. Furthermore, it was England that had propped up the slavery system! English mills consumed four-fifths of America's crop of slave-grown cotton. If England were to insist on free-grown cotton, slavery could be abolished immediately. "But are you willing to sacrifice one penny of your own profits for the sake of doing away with this cursed business?"[15] he challenged the audience. There were some scattered boos, and the next day the newspapers denounced his speech.

Calvin had struck a raw nerve. Later, when war broke out in the United States, England would have to take a stand—for or against the cotton it needed, for or against the slavery it condemned.

Finally, it was time for Calvin to return home and for Hatty and Charles to leave England. On the day before her departure, Hatty was invited to a luncheon where she met Lady Byron, the frail, beautiful widow of the great poet whose death Hatty had mourned so many years ago. Their conversation was brief, but it was the beginning of a long friendship that was to have fateful consequences in years to come.

Then it was on to France, Belgium, Switzerland, and Germany, where Hatty and Charles thoroughly enjoyed themselves visiting monuments, museums, and cathedrals. They went hiking in the Alps. And then, like many tourists before her, Hatty fell in love with Paris, where she felt a little "wicked," but "released from care."[16] In September 1853, after three months on the Continent, Hatty and Charles set sail for home, laden with gifts and testimonials. Hatty also carried with her a purse holding twenty thousand dollars given to her in the British Isles for the antislavery movement, and twenty-six leather-bound volumes containing "An Affectionate Christian Address from the Women of Great Britain to the Women of America." It was a letter, signed by more than half a million British women, calling for an end to slavery in the United States.

It was wonderful to be home again with Calvin and the children. The pretty twins, Harriet and Eliza, were seventeen now, and mischievous Georgiana was ten. Handsome, thoughtful Henry was fifteen, Frederick was thirteen, and the baby, Charles, was a rambunctious two-year-old. But there was little time to relax. Hatty recalled experiences from her recent trip and set them down in a memoir that was later published as *Sunny Memories of Foreign Lands*. The thousands of letters that had piled up in her absence also needed attention, and there were columns to be written for the *Independent*. Once again, Hatty set to work, conscious that she was regarded now as a crusader and leader in "the cause."

Across the nation, tensions over the question of slavery rose with every passing day. Violence erupted frequently, and resistance to the Fugitive Slave Act spread to such a degree that it was unenforceable in many northern states. Increasing numbers of slaves were fleeing to the North, and abolitionists stepped up their campaign to publicize the rescues of fugitives. In Congress, Illinois senator Stephen Douglas proposed his Kansas-Nebraska bill, which would, in effect, repeal the Missouri Compromise and allow slavery to spread throughout the free western territories. Out in Illinois, the news fell like a thunderbolt on a lawyer named Abraham Lincoln who decided to step out of political retirement to fight against the extension of slavery. "Slavery," he said, "is founded on the selfishness of man's nature—opposition to it in his love of justice. These principles are in eternal antagonism, and when brought into collision so fiercely as slavery extension brings them, shocks and throes and convulsions must ceaselessly follow."[17]

In May 1854, the Kansas-Nebraska bill was passed. Before long, the question of whether Kansas would enter the Union as a free or slave state would be battled out by the proslavery and antislavery settlers who were pouring into the territory.

For her part, Hatty wrote "An Appeal to the Women of America," an antislavery pamphlet. She had tens of thousands printed at her own expense, and she distributed them free of charge. She sponsored petitions to unite the Protestant clergy against slavery and sent them to her friend Charles Sumner, the abolitionist senator from Massachusetts. She doled out sums from the British funds to help the cause and continued writing scores of articles for the *Independent* and other publications.

There was time for little else. The Stowe house in Andover had become a hub of antislavery activity, with people like William Lloyd Garrison and Frederick Douglass as frequent visitors. And, too, Lyman Beecher and Catherine had come for a long stay. Now seventy-nine years old, Lyman seemed as healthy and energetic as ever, but he sometimes lapsed into incoherence and forgetfulness, so Hatty, Catherine, and their brother Charles helped the old man put together a book about his life before his memories of names and past events were forever forgotten.

The following year, at a family reunion held to celebrate the completion of Lyman's autobiography, Henry Ward described the desperate plight of the antislavery men who were trying to keep Kansas a free state. A tireless advocate of abolition, Henry Ward was famous for his fiery sermons against slavery and for rescuing slaves by bringing them to the platform of Plymouth Church where he dramatically auctioned them off to freedom. Now, a thrill went through Hatty as she listened to her brother describe how he had collected funds to buy rifles for the Free-Soldiers in Kansas and how the rifles were being shipped in barrels labeled "Bibles." Later, when the whole country knew the story, the Sharp Rifles would be nicknamed "Beecher's Bibles."

Once again, Hatty felt called to action. Pamphlets, petitions, and letters were all very fine, but they had little effect. Only a novel would allow her the scope she needed, so she set to work on a new antislavery book. This time, Hatty hoped to dramatize the evil effects of slavery on slave owners themselves. She planned to title the book *Canema*, after the plantation owned by the compassionate young slave owner who was to be the hero.

Meanwhile, the troubles in Kansas erupted into terror and violence when proslavery ruffians rode in to plunder and destroy the free-state capitol of Lawrence. A few days later, Hatty received word that her friend Charles Sumner, the antislavery senator from Massachusetts, had been brutally assaulted on the floor of the Senate by Preston Brooks, a congressman from South Carolina. As Sumner lay near death in Washington, a band of Free-Soil fighters, led by a man named John Brown, retaliated against the Lawrence massacre by killing five proslavery settlers.

Overnight, the mood of Hatty's book changed. A compassionate, slave-owning hero would no longer provide the vehicle for what she had to say. Impelled to retaliate in her own way, and writing with righteous anger, she shifted her focus to the character of Dred, an escaped slave who encourages other fugitives to take up arms against their former masters and who prophesies that only a war will put an end to slavery. And she changed the title from *Canema* to *Dred: A Tale of the Great Dismal Swamp.*

The book was published in 1856. Although her central character was possibly modeled on Nat Turner, the leader of an 1831 slave rebellion that had sent shock waves throughout the South, his name was that of a slave, Dred Scott, whose lawsuit was on its way to the Supreme Court. Scott had sued for his freedom on the grounds that his master had twice taken him into free territory. In March 1857, the court would hand down its decision in *Dred Scott* v. *Sandford,* declaring that a black person could not file a lawsuit because blacks were not, and could not be, citizens, and secondly, that the Missouri Compromise of 1820 was unconstitutional and, therefore, Congress could not prohibit slavery in the territories.

Despite its weakness, *Dred* was hailed as a masterpiece by northern readers, if not by a few critics who attacked it on political, literary, and religious grounds. But Hatty took the criticism of her new best-seller in stride. "One hundred thousand copies of 'Dred' sold in four weeks!" she wrote to Calvin. "After that who cares what critics say?"[18]

Dred promised to be equally popular in the British Isles. This time Hatty had no wish to lose her British royalties as she had with *Uncle Tom's Cabin.* Remembering how *Uncle Tom* had been pirated, and knowing that the only way to secure a British copyright was to apply for it in person, Hatty and Calvin decided to make another trip to England. They set sail in July 1856 accompanied by the twins Harriet and

Eliza (who were now twenty years old), their eldest son, Henry, and Hatty's sister, Mary Perkins.

Once again, Hatty was greeted as a celebrity. There were receptions, dinners, and meetings with prominent social and political figures. This time, however, a special thrill awaited Hatty. Queen Victoria, who ardently admired *Uncle Tom's Cabin,* wanted to meet her, so an "accidental, done on purpose meeting at a railway station" was arranged between the two most famous women in the world. "The Queen seemed really delighted to see my wife, and remarkably glad to see me for her sake," Calvin wrote in a letter to a friend. "She pointed us out to Prince Albert, who made two most gracious bows to my wife and two to me, while the four royal children stared their big blue eyes almost out looking at the little authoress of *Uncle Tom's Cabin.*" Hatty presented the Queen and Prince Albert with copies of *Dred,* and "they were soon both very busy reading. She is a real nice little body with exceedingly pleasant, kindly manners,"[19] Calvin wrote, describing the ruler of the largest, most powerful empire on earth.

After a few months in England where she met with Lady Byron and other friends, Hatty, along with her daughters and sister, continued on to France and Italy while Calvin remained in London to secure a copyright for *Dred* and arrange for publication of the book in England. His business over, he sailed for home, followed shortly by Henry who was due to begin his first year at Dartmouth College.

It was not until June 1857 that Hatty, homesick for her husband and younger children, put an end to her long holiday and returned to Andover. Only Henry was absent, but he wrote saying that he would be home as soon as his final examinations at Dartmouth were over. Hatty felt a special closeness to her handsome, intelligent son, and she looked forward to his coming. But she was never to see him again.

On July 10 came the terrible news that Henry had been drowned while swimming in the Connecticut River, and that his body was being sent to Andover. Staggered by the shock,

Hatty and Calvin could hardly believe that their fine son had been so cruelly snatched away. But so it was. Hardly aware of what they were doing, the Stowes made funeral arrangements.

All the while, Hatty was tortured by worry over Henry's spiritual state. When little Charley died nearly ten years before, Hatty had clung to her faith in God to see her through, but now she was assailed by bitter doubts. Knowing that of all people, her sister Catherine would understand her fears about Henry, Hatty wrote, "If ever I was conscious of an attack of the Devil trying to separate me from the love of Christ, it was for some days after the terrible news came. Distressing thoughts as to Henry's spiritual state were rudely thrust upon my soul. . . . I saw at last that these thoughts were . . . dishonorable to God, and that it was my duty to resist them."[20]

Grief cast a gray pall over the Stowe household. "It seems selfish that I should yearn to lie down by his side," wrote Hatty, "but I never knew how much I loved him till now."[21] Calvin spent whole days at his son's graveside, while Hatty "owled" about, as though she "were wearing an arrow that had pierced [her] heart."[22] Gradually, as she had done so many times before, Hatty found refuge in her work.

In the larger world outside Andover, the bitter controversy over slavery continued to grow.

CHAPTER 11

WAR

THE SUCCESS of *Dred,* combined with the continuing popularity of *Uncle Tom's Cabin,* made Hatty not only the most widely read but the wealthiest author in the United States. Between 1856 and 1860, her royalties averaged about six thousand dollars per month. At that time, the heads of America's largest corporations received annual salaries of about ten thousand dollars. Tuition to Harvard was fifty dollars per year, a silk dress cost less than a dollar, and bread was sold for a penny a loaf.

Yet, except for the fact that she no longer had to worry about poverty, Hatty's thrifty habits remained unchanged. She wore plain, simple clothes and refused to buy a carriage and team of horses. When visiting New York, she preferred to stay with her brother rather than spend $1.50 per day for a hotel suite. No longer forced to write "for the pay," she might have ceased working altogether, but an inner compulsion to write combined with the need to satisfy her readers drove her on.

In 1857, Hatty began a series of articles for a new magazine, *The Atlantic Monthly,* whose editor, James Russell Lowell, greatly admired her and her work. At the same time, she started a new novel and, for the first time, chose a subject other than slavery for her theme. *The Minister's Wooing,* published in 1859, "attempt[ed] to portray the heart and life of New England, its religion, theology, and manners."[1] Unable to live up to the stern dictates of Puritanism, the book's characters find that the road to salvation is like "a ladder to heaven" from which their clergymen have "knocked out every [rung] . . . but the highest, and then, pointing to its hopeless splendor, said to the world, 'Go up thither and be saved!' "[2]

Finally, Hatty had dared to express her feelings about her father's religion. Years later, her grandson, Lyman Beecher Stowe, would write, *"The Minister's Wooing* was an attack on the cruelty and injustice of Calvinism, just as *Uncle Tom's Cabin* was an attack on the cruelty and injustice of slavery. . . . She attacked Calvinism without attacking Calvinists just as . . . she attacked slavery without attacking slaveholders."[3]

To secure the British copyright for her new book, Hatty once again set sail for England, accompanied this time by Calvin and sixteen-year-old Georgiana. In her absence, *The Minister's Wooing,* with its liberating message that God is love, would gain a large audience. In England and Europe, Hatty would meet with Nathaniel Hawthorne, John Ruskin, and other friends, including Lady Byron. She would be gone for a year, away from the ever-growing bitterness that was tearing the country apart.

In 1858, Abraham Lincoln and Stephen Douglas, two Illinois candidates for the Senate, had brought the issues into sharp focus in a series of debates. "A house divided against itself cannot stand," Lincoln had proclaimed. "I believe this government cannot endure permanently, half slave and half free. . . . It will become all one thing, or all the other. . . . Either the opponents of slavery will arrest the further spread of it . . . or its advocates will push it forward till it shall become alike lawful in all the States."[4] As tensions mounted, it was no longer possible for Americans to avoid taking sides. In the North, dismay over the Dred Scott decision and the extension of slavery into the western territories impelled people to join the ranks of the abolitionists. And in the South, slave owners, who said they needed more slaves to work their newly acquired western lands, began to agitate for repeal of the federal law that prohibited the importation of slaves from Africa.

For one man, the tension became unbearable. John Brown, the gaunt, wild-eyed abolitionist who had fought for free soil in Kansas, decided that nothing could be gained by waiting for the government to act. He would organize a slave rebellion and establish a free Negro state with himself as its chief. In October 1859, Brown led a small band of zealots to Harpers Ferry, Virginia (now West Virginia), where they took several hostages, seized a federal arsenal, took a stand at the bridge that led to it, and waited for the slaves to rise in rebellion. After a fierce gunfight, a company of militia, led by Colonel Robert E. Lee, captured Brown and the remnants of his band. Although he failed to rally a single slave to insurrection, he had aroused fear and terror in southern hearts. Ten days later, John Brown was tried and sentenced by a Virginia court. A few weeks later he was hanged.

The North, overlooking the irresponsibility of Brown's raid, considered him a martyr. Ralph Waldo Emerson called him "that new saint," and Hatty, when she learned of the raid, wrote of the "brave, good man who calmly gave his life up to a noble effort for human freedom."[5] The South, however, trembled at the thought that new waves of abolitionists might be more successful at inciting slaves to rebel.

One month before Hatty returned from Europe in June 1860, the Republican Party nominated Abraham Lincoln as its presidential candidate to run against the incumbent president, James Buchanan. Hatty disagreed with Lincoln's views on abolition; time and again, he had said that he had no wish to interfere, directly or indirectly, with the institution of slavery in the states where it existed. Nevertheless, she supported his candidacy in the critical race that would determine the nation's destiny. As the division that Hatty had done so much to provoke loomed closer, Lincoln was elected president of the United States on November 6, 1860. When she learned the outcome, Hatty put aside her work to write an article expressing both gratitude and optimism. And Henry Ward, believing that Lincoln's election ended the threat that had hung over the country for so long, assured his congregation, "There will be no war!"[6] But southerners, who distrusted Lincoln's assertion that he did not mean to interfere with slavery, were engulfed by a wave of hot-tempered anger.

As the first winter snows fell in Andover, Hatty set to work on two new novels, *The Pearl of Orr's Island,* a tale set among the hardy seafaring folk of New England, which many critics consider one of her finest books, and *Agnes of Sorrento,* a romance inspired by her recent visit to Italy. Christmas came, and the house was filled with noisy activity. The news that South Carolina had voted to secede from the Union on December 20 failed to dampen Hatty's spirits. There were festive parties for the children and their friends, and Frederick, now twenty years old, set everyone laughing with his ample stock of jokes and anecdotes.

But after New Year's, there was little to be cheerful about. South Carolina's bold action had triggered a chain reaction in other states. By February 1, Alabama, Florida, Georgia, Louisiana, Mississippi, and Texas had joined South Carolina to form the Confederate States of America. On February 18, 1861, the new nation elected Jefferson Davis, the former secretary of war, as its president. In Washington, President Buchanan floundered about, seeking a compromise that would lure the seceding states back into the Union, but his efforts met with no success. Everyone wondered what would happen after Lincoln was inaugurated on March 4, 1861. The answer was not long in coming.

On April 12, Confederate forces attacked the Union outpost at Fort Sumter, a small garrison located on an island in the bay at Charleston, South Carolina. After two days of fighting, the fort was in rebel hands. Then Arkansas, North

Carolina, Tennessee, and Virginia joined the Confederacy, while West Virginia announced its separation from Virginia and declared allegiance to the Union. The Civil War had begun.

President Lincoln ordered an immediate blockade of Southern ports and called for 75,000 volunteers to fight the Confederacy. In the North, Hatty put aside her work to write for the *Independent,* "this is a cause to die for and—thanks be to God!—our young men embrace it as a bride and are ready to die."[7] Henry Ward thundered from his pulpit, "I hold that it is ten times better to have war than to have slavery."[8] And Frederick, who was studying medicine in Boston, decided that there was only one thing for a son of Harriet Beecher Stowe to do. He wasted no time in going to the recruiting office where his name was set down on the roster of Company A of the 1st Massachusetts Volunteer Infantry.

Hatty was proud of the way her handsome son, along with thousands of others, responded to the president's call for volunteers. At last the slaves would be freed! She had no way of knowing that the coming months would bring disasters and disappointments that would fill her with bewilderment and rage.

The first shock came with the news that Queen Victoria had declared that Great Britain would remain neutral in the conflict. In effect, England recognized the Confederate States of America as a separate nation. Later, England would violate its neutrality by selling battleships to the Confederacy.

Angry at England's betrayal, Hatty published an article in *The Atlantic Monthly* to appeal to the millions of British women who had signed the petition against slavery. "Sisters of England," she wrote, "it is an unaccountable fact . . . that the party which has brought the cause of freedom thus far on its way . . . has found little or no support in England. Sadder than this, the party which makes slavery the chief cornerstone of its edifice finds in England its strongest defenders."[9]

Hatty was sure she would hear from friends in the British Isles, but her article evoked little response. Nathaniel

Hawthorne wasn't surprised. "I read with great pleasure your article," he wrote to Hatty. "If anything could make John Bull blush, I should think it might be that; but he is a hardened and villainous hypocrite. I always felt that he cared nothing for or against slavery, except as it gave him a vantage-ground on which to parade his own virtue and sneer at our iniquity."[10]

Hatty couldn't help remembering that Calvin had pointed out to an audience in London how England supported slavery through its dependence on American slave-grown cotton. In a letter to the Duchess of Argyll, she wrote, "The utter failure of Christian, anti-slavery England . . . has been as bitter a grief to me as was the similar prostration of all our American religious people in the day of the Fugitive Slave Law . . . it is our agony; we tread the winepress alone, and they whose cheap rhetoric has been for years pushing us into it now desert *en masse.*"[11] She felt that she had been duped by her English "friends" all these years and vowed never to travel to the British Isles again.

Like most Northerners, Hatty viewed the Civil War as a crusade against slavery, and she believed that Union forces would put down the insurrection after a few battles. But the Confederates scored early victories. On July 21, 1861, Union troops suffered a major defeat at Manassas, Virginia, in a battle known forever after as the First Battle of Bull Run.

As hopes for a quick end to the conflict faded, Hatty grew more and more uneasy about President Lincoln's position on slavery. Lincoln had declared:

*My paramount object in this struggle is to save
the union, and is not either to save or destroy
slavery. If I could save the Union without freeing
any slave, I would do it; if I could save it by freeing all the slaves, I would do it; and if I could
save it by freeing some and leaving others alone,
I would also do that. What I do about slavery
and the colored race, I do because I believe it*

helps to save the Union; and what I forbear, I
forbear because I do not believe it would help to
save the Union.[12]

In a fierce denunciation of Lincoln's failure to declare emancipation, Hatty used her column in the *Independent* to urge
the president to action. "Now is the time," she wrote. "Now
emancipation can be given as a gift; bye-and-bye it will seem
to be wrung out as a cowardly expedient. . . . Let the President of the United States proclaim that all men shall here-
after be declared free and equal, and that the service of all
shall be accepted, without regard to color."[13] And again, she
wrote, "How long must this people wait, with this great ar-
rear of crime and injustice still unrighted?"[14]

Meanwhile, battlefield casualties continued to mount.
In 1862, the Union army was defeated in its attempt to capture Richmond, Virginia. While the Union navy seized the
Confederate ports of Roanoke, New Orleans, Galveston, and
Pensacola, bitter fighting continued to rage throughout the
Shenandoah Valley. At the Second Battle of Bull Run in August of that year, Union forces were once again crushed by
the Confederates. Hatty again urged the president to action.
"The inquisition for blood has been strict and awful," she
wrote; "The voice, *Let this people go,* has been as evident to
us as to the old Egyptians, and every refusal has been followed by defeat and plague."[15]

From the beginning, Lincoln had hoped to free the
slaves, but his plan called for legal, constitutional emancipation within the framework of a united nation. When the
war began, the preservation of the Union became his first
objective. As the devastation spread to North and South,
Lincoln waited only for some Union victory so that a proclamation of emancipation would come from a position of
strength, not weakness.

Then, in September 1862, came a terrible, bloody battle
when the rebels, commanded by General Robert E. Lee, in-
vaded Union territory and were met by Union forces at

Sharpsburg, Maryland. Before Lee's army was forced to retreat, more than twenty-four thousand soldiers lay dead or wounded at Antietam Creek.

It was a bleak victory, but it turned the tide. A few days after Antietam, Lincoln announced that he had decided on a "fit and necessary war measure for suppressing" the rebellion.[16] On January 1, 1863, he would sign an Emancipation Proclamation declaring that all slaves within states still in rebellion against the Union would be freed. In the interim, rebel states would be given the opportunity to surrender and rejoin the Union.

Like many Northerners who insisted that slavery was the central issue of the war, Hatty was angry that Lincoln had waited so long to act. Now she wondered if Lincoln truly meant what he said. In November 1862, Hatty decided to have a talk with "Father Abraham" to satisfy herself that the Emancipation Proclamation would become a reality. Taking two of her children with her, she traveled to Washington, D.C.

An interview with President Lincoln was arranged the next day. With twelve-year-old Charley at her side, Hatty entered the White House, where she was escorted to a small room that Lincoln used as a study. She was immediately drawn to the tall, awkward man with the deep, sad eyes who rose from his chair and came forward to greet her. Extending his large hand, and taking her small one in it, Lincoln said gently, "So this is the little lady who made this big war."[17] No record of their conversation exists, but they talked for an hour or more. When it was time to go, Hatty left with a strong faith in the president and a firm belief that the Emancipation Proclamation would become a reality.

Trusting that Lincoln would fulfill his promise, cities throughout the North prepared to celebrate an Emancipation Jubilee on January 1, 1863. Hatty decided to attend the Jubilee in the Boston Music Hall. From her seat high up in the balcony, she listened to selections by Mendelsohn and Beethoven. Finally, during intermission, a telegraph message came reporting that President Lincoln had just signed the Emancipation Proclamation. The words were read: "I do order and declare that all persons held as slaves within said designated States and parts of States are, and henceforward shall be, free. . . ."[18] All at once, the hall broke into tumult. People shouted and cried and kissed one another; hats and bonnets were tossed in the air. Then word spread that Hatty was in the Hall. Hands pointed her out, and with one voice, the crowd shouted, "Mrs. Stowe! Mrs. Stowe! Mrs. Stowe!" Someone guided her to the balcony rail, and with tears welling in her eyes, she looked down upon a sea of jubilant, upturned faces. Waves of applause rocked the Hall. They had not forgotten who had done the most to rouse the North to the horrors of slavery. She had written a book that had shaken the world, and now she had her reward. Hatty would always remember that splendid day. But the nation was still at war, and in the rebel states, slaves still toiled in bondage. For Hatty, the struggle would continue until every slave was free.

The sound of the ovation was still ringing in Hatty's ears when, ten days later, a telegram arrived announcing that her father was dead. For several years, Lyman Beecher had been living near Henry Ward's parsonage in Brooklyn, a thin shell of a man whose mind often wandered. He had rallied in his last moments, telling those of his children who gathered around him, "I have fought a good fight, I have finished my course."[19] Although she had long since rejected her father's stern brand of religion, Hatty mourned the death of the man who had had such a profound influence on her life. Like her brothers and sisters, she felt pride in the way Northern newspapers recalled Lyman Beecher's achievements and wit, and she found deep comfort in the belief that his soul was immortal.

Calvin Stowe, now sixty years old, was scheduled to retire from Andover Theological Seminary in the spring of 1863. Hatty was making enough money to support the family, so there was no need for Calvin to continue in work he had never enjoyed. He looked forward to writing a book on the subject that had been his chief interest for so long—the origin of the books of the Bible.

Since there would be nothing to keep them in Andover after Calvin retired, Hatty proposed that they build a house in Hartford, Connecticut. Calvin was reluctant to move, but Hatty overrode his objections and purchased four acres of woodland along the river in Hartford where she and Georgiana May had walked and dreamed so many years before. Throwing herself energetically into the project, Hatty designed the house to incorporate details of architecture she had seen abroad. She wanted arches, turrets, and gardens outside; the warmth and richness of carved wood inside. An army of workmen was hired, and the mansion began to rise. "My house with *eight* gables is growing wonderfully," she wrote. "I am busy with drains, sewers, sinks, digging, trenching, and above all with manure . . . in which the eye of faith sees Delaware grapes and d'Angouleme pears, and all sorts of roses and posies."[20] When they moved into the house the following year, the Stowes would name it "Oakholm."

Although construction of the new house occupied her time, Hatty could not dispel worries over Frederick's welfare. Twice commended for bravery in action, Frederick was now in command of a cavalry troop. Late in June 1863, General Lee and his army crossed the Potomac River and headed for Gettysburg, Pennsylvania, where Union forces, led by General Meade, were waiting. There, beginning on July 1, the bloodiest battle of the war was fought. The slaughter raged for three days before Lee and the remnants of his army finally retreated. More than forty thousand Union and Confederate soldiers lay dead, and thousands more were wounded.

Hatty's joy over the Union victory was tempered with anxiety. Like thousands of other parents, Hatty and Calvin fearfully awaited news of their son, but the scene on the battlefield was so confused that the dead, wounded, and missing could not be identified immediately. Nearly two weeks passed before Hatty received a letter informing her that "Captain Stowe ... was struck by a fragment of a shell which entered his right ear."[21]

In November 1863, Frederick left the army with a medical discharge and returned home. The family's festive homecoming celebration was spoiled, however, when Frederick arrived so intoxicated that he could scarcely speak or stand. At first, Hatty blamed her son's behavior on the painful wound that was so slow in healing, but as the days passed she resigned herself to the truth that Frederick, grandson of Lyman Beecher, who had been a founder of the temperance movement, had become an alcoholic. She prayed and begged and pleaded with Frederick to alter his self-destructive behavior, but nothing seemed to work. For years to come, Hatty would worry about her deeply troubled son and would write of "the fear, and terror, and lingering agony" of those who witnessed the "slow fulfillment of doom."[22]

As she always did in times of trial, Hatty leaned on Calvin for strength and consolation. Her husband, whom she deeply loved, had always supported her. A kind, thoughtful man, Calvin had never once shown any jealousy of her fame or any resentment at her being the family's principal breadwinner. As the years passed, he grew enormously fat, let his beard grow, and took to wearing a skullcap on his bald head. Teasingly, Hatty began to call him, "My Old Rabbi" and, if anything, the love between them seemed to grow deeper.

In 1864, they moved to Hartford. But Hatty's dream house proved to be an expensive nightmare. Throughout the six years they lived at Oakholm, something was always going wrong. Windows jammed, cellars flooded, and the plumbing didn't work. One afternoon, for instance, Calvin had just dozed off in a chair when a broken pipe caused the ceiling above him to explode. Covered with plaster, and drenched to the skin, he grumbled, "Oh yes, all the modern conveniences! Shower baths while you sleep!"[23] When repair bills were added to the cost of maintaining the house and grounds, the result was staggering. Calvin muttered dire predictions of ending up in the poorhouse.

While Calvin immersed himself in writing his book,

Hatty worked furiously to pay the ever-mounting bills. She churned out articles on a variety of subjects, ranging from the growing of camellias, home decorating, and children's stories, to child care, managing money, religion, pets, and the patriotic duty of Northerners to buy only domestically manufactured goods. Many of these pieces later appeared in book collections under the titles *House and Home Papers, Ravages of a Carpet, The Chimney Corner,* and *Little Foxes.* She also wrote a four-volume work containing biographical sketches called *Men of Our Times.* She took time out to plan her daughter Georgiana's wedding to a young minister, and to say good-bye to young Charley who had joined the crew of a commercial sailing vessel, but she was so absorbed in her work that she paid little attention to the outside world. The interminable war seemed to be going on somewhere very far away.

But on the battlefields, the carnage continued. In the west, the Confederates were defeated time and again in battles against the Union army. The genius of the campaign, a tough, brilliant general named Ulysses S. Grant, was made commander in chief of the Union forces. In March 1864, Grant came east to begin the long, costly effort to force Lee and his army into submission. The Confederates fought bravely, but as the months passed, the will to win gave way to despair. The South was devastated. Its towns and cities lay in ruins, its rich farmlands were laid waste, and its army was exhausted and starving. Then suddenly, on April 9, 1865, the long agony was over. The leaders of the two armies met at the dusty crossroads town of Appomattox Court House and there General Robert E. Lee signed the terms of surrender.

The toll was enormous for both North and South. Families had been torn apart by the deaths of fathers, sons, and brothers. Altogether, more than 620,000 Americans had laid down their lives in the bloodiest war of the nation's history. But the Union was preserved, and the slaves were free. In December, Congress would enact the Thirteenth Amendment to the Constitution, outlawing slavery forever.

Hatty was thrilled. The moment for which she had worked and waited for so long had finally arrived. But her elation was cut short when word came on April 15 that President Lincoln had been shot to death by an actor named John Wilkes Booth. As a pall of sorrow fell across the wounded land, Hatty joined with others to mourn the humble, gentle man who had suffered the trials and agonies of a nation in mortal struggle.

CHAPTER 12

A MIRROR
OF NEW ENGLAND

THE DREADFUL war was over, leaving the nation with un-answered questions. What could be done to help the former slaves find a new place in society? How would the wounded South rebuild itself?

For Hatty, the most immediate problem was how to help poor Frederick. Her hopes were raised when, one day, Frederick came home from a Hartford tavern with an exciting tale. His drinking companions had told him about opportunities in Florida where land was cheap and labor plentiful. Best of all, they had told him about a thousand-acre cotton plantation named Laurel Grove that could be rented for practically nothing. Inspired by Frederick's enthusiasm, Hatty arranged to rent the plantation, hired a hundred former slaves, and placed him in charge. Perhaps fresh air, hard work, and a change of scene would bring about the miracle she prayed for.

When Hatty visited Frederick the following winter, it seemed as though her wish had come true. The plantation buildings were unkempt, and only a few of the fields had been planted, but Frederick looked tanned and healthy in his spotless white linen suit. Best of all, he was smiling and sober.

It seemed to Hatty that it would not be difficult to be happy in this warm, beautiful land. As she breathed in the balmy air and looked about at the great live oaks hung with Spanish moss, the blossoming orange trees, the roses tumbling in wild profusion, the rich, opulent greenery, the soft white sand, she knew that she wanted to return again and again to Florida. When Frederick took her to Mandarin, a nearby village on the banks of the St. Johns River, Hatty discovered an empty cottage surrounded by orange groves which she decided to purchase.

All too soon, it was time to return to Hartford. Calvin's book, *The Origin and History of the Books of the Bible,* was finally published and, to the surprise of nearly everyone, was selling extremely well. He also published a collection of sermons and that, too, was selling nicely. The royalties from Hatty's books, added to those from Calvin's, brought in a steady income. But with the constant bills at Oakholm and the funds needed to sustain Frederick at Laurel Grove, there was never enough money. So Hatty sat down at her desk and once again started churning out articles, stories, and poems. She also began work on a new novel, *Oldtown Folks,* which she later considered the most important of her books after *Uncle Tom's Cabin,* an opinion with which most critics now agree.

Christmas came, and Hatty put aside her work as the family gathered around her at Oakholm. Georgiana and her husband were there, and so was Charles, home from the sea and ready to begin college. The cheerful, competent twins, Harriet and Eliza, decorated the house and looked after things for their mother. Only Frederick was missing, and his absence worried Hatty.

Shortly after Christmas, she decided once again to go to Florida. She would take Charles with her, and instead of traveling by sea as she had done the first time, they would make the trip on a military train. The family was concerned that "the little woman who had started the big war" would meet with hostility on the journey south. As the train moved through Virginia and the Carolinas, Hatty was shocked to see the devastation that the war had wrought. But everywhere the train stopped, Hatty was greeted with friendliness and courtesy. She was happy at this evidence that the nation's wounds were healing.

But her happiness evaporated when she and Charles arrived at Laurel Grove. They found Frederick drunk, thin, and shaky, and the plantation in shambles. Hatty stayed for three months trying to figure out a way to salvage the disaster. She had poured $10,000 into Laurel Grove, but her first concern was Frederick. She decided, at last, to pack up her son's things and bring him home. Casting about for a way to help Frederick, Hatty decided that a sea voyage might remove him from temptation and restore him in body and mind, so she coaxed Calvin into arranging a trip with his son to the Mediterranean.

In their absence, Hatty immersed herself in work. In addition to scores of articles, she finished *Oldtown Folks*. The book had taken more than two years to write and was longer, and more profound, than she had planned. Inspired by Calvin's recollections from his boyhood years in Natick, Massachusetts, Hatty had painted a shrewd, witty, and authentic portrait of New England small-town life in the early nineteenth century. She based the main character, Parson Avery, on her father, while Horace Holyoke, the narrator of the story, is none other than Calvin Stowe in disguise. "It is my résumé of the whole spirit and body of New England,"[1] Hatty wrote, and indeed, through vividly realized characters drawn from all levels of New England village life, she not only captured the humor and rhythms of Yankee talk but offered a marvelous portrayal of the intellectual and religious evolution of Puritan New England as well.

By the time Calvin and Frederick returned, Hatty was in good spirits. Frederick looked much better, but Hatty was disappointed to learn that he still had not tamed his "wild, unreasoning impulse."[2] Still hoping for a miracle, she sent him back to Florida accompanied by a cousin from the Foote side of the family to take over management of the two-hundred-acre orange grove at Mandarin. It was a wise decision. When Hatty and Calvin traveled to Florida the following winter, they found Frederick sober and the grove prospering under Spencer Foote's direction.

It was Calvin's first journey to Mandarin, and, like Hatty, he was charmed by the beauty and dreamy warmth of the place. They spent the winter in their cottage, nestled beneath the shade of a cluster of grand old live oaks on the banks of the St. Johns River. Everywhere there were flowers and birds and a sense of absolute peace, and in that idyllic place Calvin found the restful quiet his scholarly nature had always longed for. For years to come, he and Hatty would spend their winters there. Hatty's portly "old Rabbi," with his snowy, patriarchal beard and kindly face, would sit for hours in his rocking chair, immersed in his books, on the veranda overlooking the river. He became a familiar sight to travelers on the steamboats that drifted by.

Unfortunately, the Stowes' days were not always peaceful. Hatty was so famous that postcards depicting the Stowes at Mandarin were sold across the country. Tourists and souvenir hunters descended in droves, hoping for a glimpse of the nation's most famous author. Calvin, who had little patience with people who tried to invade their privacy, was often driven to shout and wave his cane angrily at intruders.

Although Florida was an Eden to Hatty, she realized that it was no paradise for the newly freed blacks who were struggling to make their way in the world. To help them in their plight, Hatty erected a small building at Mandarin to be used as a school for former slaves during the week and as a church on Sundays. During winter months, Calvin preached in the little schoolhouse and Hatty taught a variety of subjects to "the poor people" whose cause she had once defended. Their efforts drew the attention and praise of many southerners, not the least of whom was Robert E. Lee, the South's greatest hero. Hatty, the infamous northern abolitionist, had taken the South to her heart, and the South had loved her in return. She especially appreciated the affection shown by her Mandarin neighbors who, when questioned by northern tourists about where the strangers to the area lived, would reply, "There are no strangers here."[3]

The year was 1869, and *Oldtown Folks* had just been published. Hatty, now fifty-eight years old, was famous and respected throughout the world. Except for her constant worries about Frederick, she was contented and happy. Certainly she never anticipated becoming the center of a storm of criticism and controversy that would nearly ruin her public image.

Yet that is what happened. One day, while browsing through new books at a booksellers, Hatty came across the memoirs of the Countess Teresa Guiccioli, Byron's last mistress. Ever since childhood, Hatty had been fascinated by the wild, romantic poet. Before meeting Lady Byron, Hatty had heard all the gossip—that the poet's widow was a cruel, coldhearted woman, incapable of understanding her husband's genius, and that by taking their child and leaving him after one year of marriage, she had driven the poet to reckless despair. After their separation, Byron led a dissolute life on the continent, drinking heavily, gambling, and pursuing a succession of lovers, until his untimely death.

The Anne Byron that Hatty knew, however, was a reserved, intelligent woman. The two women had become intimate friends almost instantly, and in the course of their long conversations, Anne Byron gradually revealed a terrible, dark secret about her dead husband. Now, as she read Countess Guiccioli's book, Hatty's anger rose. Once again, Anne Byron was being blamed for the storm of scandalous stories that had surrounded the dead poet. But Anne, who had spent her life suffering similar attacks in silence, had died nine years before. Hatty, seeing "these foul slanders crystallizing into history,"[4] decided to rise to her friend's defense and tell the world, at long last, the dreadful truth about Lord Byron.

And what was the truth? From Anne Byron, Hatty had

learned that Lord Byron, whom the world remembered as a noble, sensitive poet, was in reality a philandering, depraved drunkard who, before his marriage, had been involved in an incestuous relationship with his half sister, and that, as a result of their unholy union, an illegitimate child had been born.

In an article defending Anne and refuting the Countess Guiccioli's claims, Hatty used guarded language to reveal the explosive confidence. "He fell into the depths of a secret adulterous intrigue with a blood relation, so near in consanguinity that discovery must have been utter ruin and expulsion from civilized society." That secret, she wrote, explained Byron's later behavior. "From henceforth this damning guilty secret became the ruling force in his life, holding him with morbid fascination, yet filling him with remorse and anguish and insane dread of detection."[5]

Fearing that her action would tarnish her own name and reputation, Calvin pleaded with Hatty not to publish the article. But Hatty was fiercely determined to redeem her friend's good name. In August 1869, "The True Story of Lady Byron's Life" was published in the *Atlantic Monthly*. The result was a catastrophic storm of criticism. In both England and the United States, incensed readers reacted as though Hatty had written an obscene piece of pornography about the wild, reckless poet who was a romantic ideal to millions of people. The *Atlantic Monthly* lost thousands of subscribers because of Hatty's article, while magazines and newspapers attacked her with a flood of articles and cartoons painting her as an evil, malicious old gossip who had dared to fling mud on the sacred memory of a noble genius. Dubbing Hatty "a mere sensationalist writer," a United States congressman offered an apology to Great Britain, claiming "nothing from her pen is considered reliable by the American public."[6] And in England, the House of Commons debated a proposal that Hatty be barred for life from visiting the British Isles.

Just as *Uncle Tom's Cabin* had done, the article provoked a spate of books rebutting Hatty's charges and attacking her integrity. And just as she had done before with *A Key to Uncle Tom's Cabin*, Hatty decided to write a book justifying her position. Calvin and her family begged her to let the controversy die down, but Hatty refused; she was a Beecher, and no Beecher backed away from a fight. She could not believe that people would accept "the story of an avowed libertine against that of a pure, noble woman whose whole life shows not one record of duty unfulfilled."[7] She assembled a vast amount of evidence corroborating the view that Byron was, indeed, mentally unstable and an abusive husband. In writing the book, she charged that her critics defended Lord Byron because he was a man, and that her word and Lady Byron's were discounted because they were women.

The book was published in 1870 as *Lady Byron Vindicated*, and once again Hatty was attacked by the critics. Among the few who rose to her defense was the feminist leader, Elizabeth Cady Stanton, who believed that Hatty's book would "hasten the day when the worst form of slavery, that of woman to man, that has ever cursed the earth, shall be no more."[8] Hatty could not stand by when injustices were committed. Just as she had risen to the defense of the slaves years before, she now rose to the defense of women in the person of Lady Byron. And if Hatty ever regretted writing either the article or the book, she never said so.

In 1871, the storm over *Lady Byron Vindicated* gradually died down, but the long, angry controversy had taken its toll. Now sixty years old, Hatty was tired. Nearly twenty years had passed since *Uncle Tom's Cabin* had made her world famous, and she had written a vast body of work since then. She needed a rest and was ill-prepared for the blow that was about to fall.

Frederick, who was still fighting his lonely battle against alcoholism, wrote to say that since he was contributing little to the operation of the Mandarin groves, he had signed on for a voyage around Cape Horn to Chile, where he hoped to make a new start. Although she didn't know it, this was the last letter Hatty was ever to receive from her beloved soldier boy.

Much later, Hatty and Calvin learned that Frederick had not debarked in Chile but had stayed aboard the ship until it reached San Francisco, where he had gone ashore and vanished without a trace. Did he commit suicide? Was he murdered? Or had he run away to avoid disgracing those he loved? Although the police investigated Frederick's disappearance, no clues were ever found.

If they had been certain that Frederick was dead, Hatty and Calvin would have accepted the fact. But not knowing what had happened to their son was a daily torment from which they could never escape. Hatty buried her grief deep inside herself, and to the end of her days, she never ceased to hope that Frederick would return. But the tragedy changed her forever. Although she would go on to write nearly a dozen more books, the spontaneity and passionate intensity that inspired her earlier writings were gone.

After Frederick's disappearance, Hatty finally realized that it was time to give up Oakholm. A factory was being built within sight of the house, the nearby river was polluted, and the cost of maintaining the house remained exorbitant. In 1873, she put the house up for sale and purchased a new, smaller house on Forest Street in Hartford. Next door lived an up-and-coming young author named Samuel L. Clemens, whom the world would know as Mark Twain. Before long, a friendship developed between the Stowes and Mark Twain, who found the older couple full of the wit and humor that he himself so much enjoyed.

Hatty, as always, continued to write books. These included three novels—*Pink and White Tyranny, My Wife and I,* and *We and Our Neighbors*—about life in a large city; a collection of sketches called *Old Town Fireside Stories;* two children's books; and a book about Biblical heroines entitled *Women in Sacred History.* Despite the Byron furor, Hatty's readers never deserted her and her books sold well. In 1873, she published *Palmetto Leaves,* a collection of sketches and essays about Florida, which not only became an overnight bestseller but also spurred a real estate boom in Florida. She also helped her sister Catherine, now in her seventies, to write two books about housekeeping and domestic science. And she tried to settle arguments between family members and her increasingly eccentric half-sister, Isabella Beecher Hooker, who was involved in the women's suffrage movement.

It was one of Isabella's friends, Victoria Woodhull, who set off a scandal that was to hurt Hatty and her family more deeply than even the Byron affair. Woodhull, a radical activist in the women's rights movement, was a frank advocate of "free love," the notion that it was morally acceptable to have sexual relations outside of marriage. And it was Woodhull upon whom Hatty had based the character of Audacia Dangereyes, a woman of questionable morals, in her book, *My Wife and I.*

Whether Woodhull was reacting to Hatty's unflattering portrait, or whether something else sparked her attack is still unclear. Whatever the cause, Woodhull sent a letter to the New York *World* in 1871 stating that, "my judges preach against 'free love' openly, and practice it secretly. For example, I know of one man, a public teacher of eminence, who lives in concubinage with the wife of another public teacher of almost equal eminence."[9] The "teacher of eminence" to whom she referred was none other than Hatty's brother, Henry Ward Beecher.

A pillar of Protestantism, the champion of a half-dozen reform movements, and easily the most popular preacher in America, Henry Ward routinely mesmerized his congregation at the Plymouth Church in Brooklyn with his brilliant oratory. In constant demand as a speaker throughout the United States and Great Britain, he commanded higher fees than any other lecturer of the time. He lived with his wife and ten children in a comfortable house where he entertained some of the most prominent people of the time. No hint of scandal had ever touched his name.

Rumors began to spread, but few people believed them. Then, in 1872, Victoria Woodhull published an article openly accusing Henry Ward of carrying on an adulterous affair with Elizabeth Tilton, the wife of Theodore Tilton, one of Henry Ward's closest friends and a member of his congregation. For more than a year, Theodore Tilton did nothing, but in December 1873, he swore out a civil complaint charging Henry Ward Beecher with having alienated his wife's affections, and demanding $100,000 as recompense. The sensational trial, which dragged on for months, became the scandal of the century. In the end, Henry Ward was acquitted. Although the jury had not reached a unanimous verdict, most people believed that Henry Ward Beecher was vindicated.

When the scandal broke, Hatty was shocked and outraged at the idea that anyone could believe the scandalous accusations made against her beloved brother. She was convinced that the plot to ruin him had been concocted by jealous enemies. "My brother," she wrote to her friend, the novelist George Eliot, "is hopelessly generous and confiding. His inability to believe evil is something incredible, and so has come all this suffering. . . . This has drawn on my life—my heart's blood . . . I felt a blow at him more than at myself."[10]

With unwavering faith in Henry Ward's innocence, Hatty stood by him, as did the entire Beecher clan—except for Isabella, who was sure of her half-brother's guilt. When Isabella, whom many people regarded as unbalanced, announced her intention to denounce Henry Ward from the pulpit of the Plymouth Church, Hatty knew she must act. Hatty was the only one in the family who had the power to awe Isabella. So, week after week, she stationed herself in a front pew during services in the Plymouth Church, ready to silence Isabella with a stern look if she dared to appear. Afraid of her older sister, Isabella backed down, but Hatty refused to speak to her ever again.

Throughout Henry Ward's long ordeal, Hatty continued to work as hard as ever, but her energy was wearing thin. "I feel like a poor old woman I once read about," she wrote to one of her daughters,

> " 'Who always was tired
> 'Cause she lived in a house
> Where help wasn't hired,'

"and of whom it is related that in her dying moments

> " 'She folded her hands
> With the latest endeavor,
> Saying nothing, dear nothing,
> Sweet nothing forever.'

"I luxuriate in laziness. I don't want to do anything or go anywhere."[11]

Hatty was certainly entitled to a rest, but when a lecture bureau proposed that she make a tour of New England with a program of readings from her books, she embraced the idea with customary enthusiasm. Although she was sixty-one years old and had never delivered a public speech in her life, she was sure it would be easy. After all, wasn't she a Beecher, that tribe of distinguished orators? Besides, the compensation offered by the lecture bureau was generous, and she could use the money.

At her first appearance, Hatty was so gripped with stage fright that she lost her voice. But failure, it seemed, was just what she needed to pull herself together. Before her next reading, she stood before a mirror and combed her white hair into a high crest such as Lyman Beecher had worn. Turning to a friend, Hatty said, "Now my dear, gaze upon me. I am exactly like my father when he was going to preach."[12] Then, imitating one of Lyman's dramatic gestures, she stepped onto the stage and read from *Uncle Tom's Cabin* with such emotional intensity that even children in the audience could not fail to understand how her words had helped to lead a generation through the struggles of war.

Without Hatty by his side, Calvin slipped easily into his old hypochondria and wrote to her that he feared he had not long to live. "Try to remain with us yet a while longer,"[13] Hatty replied teasingly. Although she missed her husband, she liked speaking before packed houses and enjoyed the roaring applause that followed. The next year, she made another tour that took her through Illinois and Ohio. But the "fearful distances and wretched trains" and "the strain of that awful journey"[14] took their toll. She decided to put an end to her speaking career.

For the next few years, the pattern of Hatty's life was set, with winters in Mandarin and summers in Hartford. The twins, Harriet and Eliza, had remained unmarried and continued to look after both homes. Georgiana and her husband had produced a wonderful grandson named Freeman. And Charles, the youngest, had become a minister and was now married.

With her children all grown, Hatty began to think of her own childhood. Drawing on recollections of the happy old days in Litchfield and Nut Plains, she began to write her last novel. In the story, Litchfield became "Poganuc," and the book itself was titled *Poganuc People.* She made the heroine like herself, the daughter of a minister who grows up in the bleak atmosphere of Calvinism but finds, in the end, a warmer, more human faith in the embrace of the Episcopal Church. And she filled the book with lively Yankee characters and drawling Yankee wit, and with nostalgia for a New England that had vanished long ago. Then, just as she was finishing the book, word came that her sister Catherine, aged seventy-eight, had died. Hatty was getting old herself, and after a lifetime of writing to support her family and to fight injustice, perhaps it was time to take a rest. She would go on to write letters, articles, and a children's story entitled *A Dog's Mission,* which Mark Twain displayed prominently in his library. But *Poganuc People,* published in 1878, would be her last full-length novel.

One last public triumph awaited Hatty. It came on her

seventy-first birthday in 1882, when her publishers, Messrs. Houghton, Mifflin & Company of Boston, honored her with a garden party to which they invited more than two hundred of America's most illustrious literary men and women. In the bright June sunshine, a band played, refreshments were served on the lawn, and more than a score of well-known authors, including John Greenleaf Whittier and Dr. Oliver Wendell Holmes, read poems and speeches composed in her honor. Henry Ward was there, too, with a warm, emotional tribute. Telegrams and letters of congratulation were read and, finally, the celebration ended with a few words from Hatty herself. The whole company rose, and remained standing until she was finished. In her quiet, modest way, she talked with optimism of the progress being made by former slaves in the South. She told how she and Calvin had seen black men acquiring property, becoming educated, and assuming responsibilities. "Just remember that this great sorrow of slavery has gone, gone by forever," she said. And then, echoing the old Calvinist faith, she added, "Let us never doubt. Everything that ought to happen is going to happen."[15]

Suddenly, or so it seemed to Hatty, both she and Calvin were old. By 1884, they found traveling too difficult and gave up their winters in Florida. Then Calvin fell ill, truly ill, and Hatty spent her days at his side, reading, talking, or simply holding his hand in silence. There were daily visits from the children. And Mark Twain, who was fond of Hatty and the "old professor," often dropped in with jokes and stories to amuse them. On August 6, 1886, Hatty's "old Rabbi" fell quietly into his final sleep. He was buried in the cemetery at Andover, close to their son Henry.

There were more sorrows the following year. In February, Henry Ward suffered a stroke and died within a week. Still, it made no sense to weep and mourn. Her beloved brother, she believed, had gone to a higher, more glorious life, along with so many of those she had loved.

After Calvin's death, the pressures that had kept Hatty

going for so many years seemed to lift. She wondered what to do, what purpose she had yet to fulfill. "I feel about all things now as I do about the things that happen in a hotel, after my trunk is packed to go home," she wrote to her brother Edward. "I may be vexed and annoyed—but what of it! I am going home soon."[16]

Her thoughts often drifted over the past and she decided to leave behind "some recollections of my life."[17] With her son Charles's help, she gathered her papers together and, in 1889, *The Life of Harriet Beecher Stowe; Compiled from Her Letters and Journals by Her Son, Charles Edward Stowe* was published. "I am going to my Father's and tho with great difficulty, I am got hither, yet now, I do not repent me of all the troubles I have been at to arrive where I am," she wrote in the foreword. "My sword I give to him that shall succeed me in my pilgrimage, and my courage and skill to him that can get it." She signed it, "Hartford, September 30, 1889, Harriet Beecher Stowe," the way Calvin had advised her to so many years ago. It was her final farewell to her readers.

Soon after that, Hatty suffered a mild stroke which left her changed. Her body recovered, but her thoughts wandered out of control. In 1893, she wrote to Oliver Wendell Holmes, "I make no mental effort of any sort; my brain is tired out. It was a woman's brain and not a man's, and finally from sheer fatigue and exhaustion in the march and strife of life it gave out before the end was reached. And now I rest me, like a moored boat, rising and falling on the water, with loosened cordage and flapping sail."[18]

She spent her days among the flowers in the garden, looking over books of pictures, or taking long, rambling walks about the neighborhood. She loved to listen to music. "I could not have too much of it," she said, "and I never *do* have as much as I should like."[19]

Sometimes Hatty seemed to forget who and where she was. Very early one morning, Mark Twain was awakened when Hatty wandered into his house and began to sing hymns and play the organ loudly in his parlor. Later, Twain recalled that "she was able to deal in surprises, and she liked to do it. She would slip up behind a person who was deep in dreams and musings and fetch a war whoop that would jump that person out of his clothes."[20]

One day, a strange gentleman approached Hatty on the street. He had read *Uncle Tom's Cabin* and wished to shake hands with its author. She seemed perplexed at first, but gradually a light dawned in her eyes. "Ah yes," she said, smiling, "that was a great book. God wrote it."

Of all her past sorrows, one never ceased haunting her. She was certain that Frederick, who had vanished more than twenty years before, would return soon. She often came back from her rambles laden with flowers to decorate the house for his homecoming, and whenever she saw someone dressed in uniform, she would dart up to him, hoping to find her long-lost son.

She was a frail, wistful, little woman, but it was hard for Harriet and Eliza to keep up with her, so they hired a nurse to be her companion. Then came the time when she no longer had strength to move from her bed. Near midnight, on July 1, 1896, two weeks after her eighty-fifth birthday, she smiled at her nurse and whispered, "I love you." Then she lay back on her pillow, and as simply as that, Hatty Beecher Stowe shed the chains of life and was gone into final freedom.

Of all her children, only the twins and Charles were left to stand beside Hatty's grave when they buried her in the Andover Chapel Cemetery between Calvin and her son Henry. She had always loved flowers, and there were mounds of them, including a wreath that bore a card from "The Children of Uncle Tom," sent by former slaves in Boston.

LEGACY TO A NATION

WHEN HARRIET BEECHER STOWE died, millions of people around the world mourned the passing of the sensitive, imaginative, and extraordinarily intelligent woman whose New England Puritanism had driven her into the battle against slavery. She left behind a massive body of writing including numerous articles, stories, letters, and tracts, and more than thirty books, including her masterpiece, *Uncle Tom's Cabin.*

To this day, *Uncle Tom's Cabin* is the book people think they know, even if they haven't read it, because characters and scenes from it have become part of our folklore and language. This is due in large part to the theater versions of *Uncle Tom's Cabin* that mushroomed in the United States and the British Isles soon after the book was published in 1852.

Unfortunately, Harriet Beecher Stowe had failed to secure dramatic rights to the book, so she had no control over the stage adaptations. The Tom shows, as they were called, proved to be highly popular with audiences well into the twentieth century, but the plot, characters, and meaning of the book were distorted. For instance, in the stage melodramas, Eliza was pursued across the frozen river by yelping bloodhounds (there are no bloodhounds in the book); little Eva was hauled heavenward by a pulley; the pathetic slave, Topsy, became a comic character who "just growed,"; and Uncle Tom, whom Stowe had painted as a black Christ, was portrayed as a pious fool, the sad symbol of a servile black American, who was whipped to death by a white man.

In this manner, the book that championed an oppressed people gradually came to stand as a symbol of that oppression. Because of the continuing confusion between the book and the plays, these distortions persist today. In 1976, the black writer, James Baldwin, would condemn the book and sneer at its author for creating a character "robbed of his humanity and divested of his sex."[1] And our dictionaries continue to define "Uncle Tom" as a black who is "humiliatingly subservient or deferential to whites."

Despite the misunderstandings and misconceptions surrounding it, *Uncle Tom's Cabin* remains a profound, powerful work, as fresh and exciting as it was nearly 150 years ago when the great Russian writer, Leo Tolstoy, declared it was among the great achievements of the human mind. Certainly, "that triumphant work," as the novelist Henry James called it, still has "the extraordinary fortune of finding itself, for an immense number of people, much less a book than a state of vision, of feeling and of consciousness."[2]

Her life, no less than her famous book, rendered Harriet Beecher Stowe a permanent place in the hearts of Americans. As her friend, the poet Elizabeth Barrett Browning, remarked, "She above all women (yes, and men of the age) has moved the world—and *for good.*" Another contemporary, the novelist George Sand, wrote, "she has genius as humanity feels the need of genius,—the genius of goodness, not that of the man of letters, but that of the saint."[3]

But Stowe claimed no genius or special goodness. Her staunch New England principles demanded that she honor simple virtues and fight for equality for all people—black and white, women and men. She was always modest, always humble, and always did as her faith decreed. "If there had been a grand preparatory blast of trumpets or had it been announced that Mrs. Stowe would do this or that," she once said, "I think it likely I could not have written; but nobody expected anything . . . and so I wrote freely."[4]

SOURCE NOTES

Chapter One: A New England Childhood

1. Johanna Johnston, *Runaway to Heaven.* New York: Doubleday & Co., Inc., 1963, p. 4.
2. ibid., p. 4.
3. ibid., p. 5.
4. Charles Edward Stowe, *The Life of Harriet Beecher Stowe.* Boston: Houghton Mifflin Co., 1889, p. 3.
5. ibid., p. 4.
6. ibid., p. 4.
7. Noel B. Gerson, *Harriet Beecher Stowe.* New York: Praeger Publishers, Inc., 1976, p. 4.
8. Charles Edward Stowe, *The Life of Harriet Beecher Stowe.* Boston: Houghton Mifflin Co., 1889, p. 8.
9. ibid., p. 8.
10. ibid., p. 8.
11. ibid., p. 9.
12. ibid., p. 10.
13. ibid., p. 11.
14. ibid., p. 13.
15. ibid., p. 14.
16. ibid., p. 14.

Chapter Two: School and Church

1. Johanna Johnston, *Runaway to Heaven.* New York: Doubleday & Co., Inc., p. 23.
2. Charles Edward Stowe, *The Life of Harriet Beecher Stowe.* Boston: Houghton Mifflin Co., 1889, p. 9.
3. Johanna Johnston, *Runaway to Heaven.* New York: Doubleday & Co., Inc., 1963, p. 31.
4. ibid., p. 31.
5. Charles Edward Stowe, *The Life of Harriet Beecher Stowe.* Boston: Houghton Mifflin Co., 1889, p. 29.
6. ibid., p. 30.
7. ibid., p. 31.
8. ibid., p. 31.
9. ibid., p. 32.
10. ibid., p. 32.
11. ibid., p. 33.
12. ibid., p. 33.
13. ibid., p. 34.
14. ibid., p. 34.
15. ibid., p. 35.
16. ibid., p. 36.
17. ibid., p. 37.
18. ibid., p. 37.
19. ibid., p. 38.
20. ibid., p. 38.
21. Johanna Johnston, *Runaway to Heaven.* New York: Doubleday & Co., Inc., 1963, p. 53.
22. ibid., p. 54.
23. Robert E. Jakoubek, *Harriet Beecher Stowe.* New York: Chelsea House, 1989, p. 32.
24. Charles Edward Stowe, *The Life of Harriet Beecher Stowe.* Boston: Houghton Mifflin Co., 1889, p. 48.
25. ibid., p. 50.
26. Johanna Johnston, *Runaway to Heaven.* New York: Doubleday & Co., Inc., 1963, p. 63.

Chapter Three: Cincinnati

1. Charles Edward Stowe, *The Life of Harriet Beecher Stowe.* Boston: Houghton Mifflin Co., 1889, p. 46.
2. ibid., p. 52.
3. Johanna Johnston, *Runaway to Heaven.* New York: Doubleday & Co., Inc., 1963, p. 62.
4. Noel B. Gerson, *Harriet Beecher Stowe: A Biography.* New York: Praeger Publishers, Inc., 1976, p. 23.
5. Charles Edward Stowe, *The Life of Harriet Beecher Stowe.* Boston: Houghton Mifflin Co., 1889, p. 56.
6. ibid., p. 58.
7. Charles Dickens, *American Notes.* New York: Oxford University Press, 1986, p. 192.
8. Charles Edward Stowe, *The Life of Harriet Beecher Stowe.* Boston: Houghton Mifflin Co., 1889, p. 63.
9. Johanna Johnston, *Runaway to Heaven.* New York: Doubleday & Co., Inc., 1963, p. 91.
10. ibid., p. 92.
11. Charles Edward Stowe, *The Life of Harriet Beecher Stowe.* Boston: Houghton Mifflin Co., 1889, p. 67.
12. Johanna Johnston, *Runaway to Heaven.* New York: Doubleday & Co., Inc., 1963, p. 99.
13. Noel B. Gerson, *Harriet Beecher Stowe.* New York: Praeger Publishers, Inc., 1976, p. 35.

Chapter Four: Witness to Slavery

1. Harriet Beecher Stowe, *A Key to Uncle Tom's Cabin.* Port Washington, NY: Kennikat Press, Inc., 1968, p. 47.
2. Charles Edward Stowe, *The Life of Harriet Beecher Stowe.* Boston: Houghton Mifflin Co., 1889, p. 71.
3. Johanna Johnston, *Runaway to Heaven.* New York: Doubleday & Co., Inc., 1963, p. 109.
4. ibid., p. 109.
5. Charles Edward Stowe, *The Life of Harriet Beecher Stowe.* Boston: Houghton Mifflin Co., 1889, p. 75.
6. Johanna Johnston, *Runaway to Heaven.* New York: Doubleday & Co., Inc., 1963, p. 112.

Chapter Five: Calvin Stowe

1. Johanna Johnston, *Runaway to Heaven*. New York: Doubleday
   & Co., Inc., 1963, p. 122.
2. Robert E. Jakoubek, *Harriet Beecher Stowe*. New York: Chelsea
   House, 1989, p. 40.
3. Johanna Johnston, *Runaway to Heaven*. New York: Doubleday
   & Co., Inc., 1963, p. 128.
4. ibid., p. 128.
5. Charles Edward Stowe, *The Life of Harriet Beecher Stowe*. Boston: Houghton Mifflin Co., pp. 76–77.
6. ibid., pp. 78–79.

Chapter Six: The Young Mrs. Stowe

1. Charles Edward Stowe, *The Life of Harriet Beecher Stowe*. Boston: Houghton Mifflin Co., 1889, pp. 80–81.
2. ibid., p. 83.
3. ibid., p. 85.
4. ibid., p. 88.
5. ibid., p. 89.
6. ibid., pp. 90–92.
7. Johanna Johnston, *Runaway to Heaven*. New York: Doubleday
   & Co., Inc., 1963, p. 158.
8. ibid., p. 157.
9. Charles Edward Stowe, *The Life of Harriet Beecher Stowe*. Boston: Houghton Mifflin Co., 1889, pp. 94–95.
10. ibid., p. 98.

Chapter Seven: Poverty, Sickness, and Sorrow

1. Charles Edward Stowe, *The Life of Harriet Beecher Stowe*. Boston: Houghton Mifflin Co., 1889, p. 101.
2. ibid., p. 103.
3. ibid., p. 104.
4. ibid., p. 102.
5. ibid., p. 106.
6. ibid., p. 104.
7. ibid., p. 107.
8. ibid., p. 108.

9. ibid., p. 110.
10. Noel B. Gerson, *Harriet Beecher Stowe.* New York: Praeger Publishers, 1976, p. 56.
11. Charles Edward Stowe, *The Life of Harriet Beecher Stowe.* Boston: Houghton Mifflin Co., 1889, p. 111.
12. ibid., p. 112.
13. ibid., p. 114.
14. ibid., p. 118.
15. ibid., p. 119.
16. ibid., p. 120.
17. ibid., p. 122.
18. ibid., p. 123–24.
19. ibid., p. 124.

Chapter Eight: "I Will Write That Thing!"

1. James M. McPherson, *Battle Cry of Freedom.* New York: Oxford University Press, Inc., 1988, p. 42.
2. Charles Edward Stowe, *The Life of Harriet Beecher Stowe.* Boston: Houghton Mifflin Co., 1889, p. 132.
3. ibid., p. 139.
4. James M. McPherson, *Battle Cry of Freedom.* New York: Oxford University Press, 1988, p. 82.
5. ibid., p. 82.
6. Charles Edward Stowe, *The Life of Harriet Beecher Stowe.* Boston: Houghton Mifflin Co., 1889, p. 145.
7. ibid., p. 145.
8. ibid., p. 146.
9. ibid., p. 146.

Chapter Nine: *Uncle Tom's Cabin*

1. Johanna Johnston, *Runaway to Heaven.* New York: Doubleday & Co., Inc., 1963, p. 200.
2. Charles Edward Stowe, *The Life of Harriet Beecher Stowe.* Boston: Houghton Mifflin Co., 1889, p. 148.
3. ibid., p. 149.
4. Johanna Johnston, *Runaway to Heaven.* New York: Doubleday & Co., Inc., 1963, p. 203.
5. ibid., pp. 203–4.

6. Charles Edward Stowe, *The Life of Harriet Beecher Stowe*. Boston: Houghton Mifflin Co., 1889, p. 150.
7. Johanna Johnston, *Runaway to Heaven*. New York: Doubleday & Co., Inc., 1963, p. 237.
8. Harriet Beecher Stowe, *Uncle Tom's Cabin*. New York: Viking Penguin Inc., 1981, p. 298.
9. Johanna Johnston, *Runaway to Heaven*. New York: Doubleday & Co., Inc., 1963, p. 223.

Chapter Ten: In the Eye of a Storm

1. Charles Edward Stowe, *The Life of Harriet Beecher Stowe*. Boston: Houghton Mifflin Co., 1889, pp. 197–98.
2. ibid., p. 162.
3. ibid., p. 161.
4. Noel B. Gerson, *Harriet Beecher Stowe*. New York: Praeger Publishers, 1976, p. 72.
5. Johanna Johnston, *Runaway to Heaven*. New York: Doubleday & Co., Inc., 1963, p. 225.
6. Charles Edward Stowe, *The Life of Harriet Beecher Stowe*. Boston: Houghton Mifflin Co., 1889, p. 182.
7. ibid., p. 181.
8. ibid., pp. 180–81.
9. ibid., p. 181.
10. ibid., p. 187.
11. James M. McPherson, *Battle Cry of Freedom*. New York: Oxford University Press, 1988, p. 90.
12. Harriet Beecher Stowe, *A Key to Uncle Tom's Cabin*. Port Washington, NY: Kennikat Press, Inc., 1968, pp. iii–iv.
13. Johanna Johnston, *Runaway to Freedom*. New York: Doubleday & Co., Inc., 1963, p. 274.
14. Noel B. Gerson, *Harriet Beecher Stowe*. New York: Praeger Publishers, 1976, p. 94.
15. Johnston, *Runaway to Heaven*, p. 278.
16. Gerson, *Harriet Beecher Stowe*, p. 96.
17. Abraham Lincoln, *Speeches and Letters of Abraham Lincoln, 1832–1865*. New York: E. P. Dutton & Co., 1907, p. 32.
18. Charles Edward Stowe, *The Life of Harriet Beecher Stowe*. Boston: Houghton Mifflin Co., 1889, p. 279.

19. ibid., p. 271.
20. ibid., p. 322.
21. ibid., p. 323.
22. ibid., p. 320.

Chapter Eleven: War

1. Charles Edward Stowe, *The Life of Harriet Beecher Stowe.* Boston: Houghton Mifflin Co., 1889, p. 343.
2. Charles H. Foster, *The Rungless Ladder: Harriet Beecher Stowe and New England Puritanism.* Durham, NC: Duke University Press, 1954, p. iv.
3. Lyman Beecher Stowe, *Saints, Sinners, and Beechers.* Indianapolis: The Bobbs-Merrill Company, 1934, p. 202.
4. Abraham Lincoln, *Speeches and Letters of Abraham Lincoln, 1832–1865.* New York: E. P. Dutton & Co., 1907, p. 69.
5. Johanna Johnston, *Runaway to Freedom.* New York: Doubleday & Co., Inc., 1963, p. 333.
6. ibid., p. 342.
7. ibid., p. 347.
8. ibid., p. 346.
9. Charles Edward Stowe, *The Life of Harriet Beecher Stowe.* Boston: Houghton Mifflin Co., 1889, pp. 384–89.
10. ibid., p. 394.
11. ibid., p. 370.
12. Abraham Lincoln, *Speeches and Letters of Abraham Lincoln, 1832–1865.* New York: E. P. Dutton & Co., 1907, p. 195.
13. Johanna Johnston, *Runaway to Freedom.* New York: Doubleday & Co., Inc., 1963, p. 352.
14. ibid., p. 353.
15. ibid., p. 353.
16. ibid., p. 355.
17. ibid., p. 357.
18. Abraham Lincoln, *Speeches and Letters of Abraham Lincoln, 1832–1865.* New York: E. P. Dutton & Co., 1907, p. 204.
19. Noel B. Gerson, *Harriet Beecher Stowe.* New York: Praeger Publishers, 1976, p. 171.
20. Johanna Johnston, *Runaway to Freedom.* New York: Doubleday & Co., Inc., 1963, p. 360.

21. Charles Edward Stowe, *The Life of Harriet Beecher Stowe.* Boston: Houghton Mifflin Co., 1889, p. 372.
22. Johanna Johnston, *Runaway to Freedom.* New York: Doubleday & Co., Inc., 1963, p. 370.
23. ibid., p. 384.

Chapter Twelve: A Mirror of New England

1. Noel B. Gerson, *Harriet Beecher Stowe.* New York: Praeger Publishers, 1976, p. 177.
2. Johanna Johnston, *Runaway to Freedom.* New York: Doubleday & Co., Inc., 1963, p. 396.
3. Gerson, *Harriet Beecher Stowe*, p. 181.
4. Charles Edward Stowe, *The Life of Harriet Beecher Stowe.* Boston: Houghton Mifflin Co., 1889, p. 446.
5. Johnston, *Runaway to Freedom*, p. 402.
6. Gerson, *Harriet Beecher Stowe*, p. 186.
7. Johnston, *Runaway to Freedom*, p. 407.
8. Elizabeth Ammons, *Critical Essays on Harriet Beecher Stowe.* Boston: G. K. Hall & Co., 1980, p. 175.
9. Johanna Johnston, *Runaway to Freedom.* New York: Doubleday & Co., Inc., 1963, p. 431.
10. Charles Edward Stowe, *The Life of Harriet Beecher Stowe.* Boston: Houghton Mifflin Co., 1889, pp. 478–80.
11. ibid., pp. 489–90.
12. Johnston, *Runaway to Freedom*, p. 440.
13. Stowe, *The Life of Harriet Beecher Stowe*, p. 492.
14. Stowe, p. 499.
15. Stowe, pp. 506–7.
16. Stowe, p. 512.
17. Stowe, p. i.
18. Johnston, *Runaway to Freedom*, p. 472.
19. Johnston, p. 472.
20. Charles H. Foster, *The Rungless Ladder: Harriet Beecher Stowe and New England Puritanism.* Durham, NC: Duke University Press, 1954, p. 162.

Epilogue

1. Elizabeth Ammons, *Critical Essays on Harriet Beecher Stowe.* Boston: G. K. Hall & Co., 1980, p. 139.

2. ibid., p. 286.
3. Annie Fields, editor, *The Life and Letters of Harriet Beecher Stowe.* Boston: Houghton Mifflin Co., 1898, p. 154.
4. David McCullough, *Brave Companions.* Englewood Cliffs, NJ: Prentice-Hall Press, 1992, p. 51.

BIBLIOGRAPHY

Adams, J. R. *Harriet Beecher Stowe*. New York: Twayne Publishers, Inc., 1963.

Ammons, Elizabeth. *Critical Essays on Harriet Beecher Stowe*. Boston: G. K. Hall & Co., 1980.

Blassingame, John W., editor. *Slave Testimony*. Baton Rouge, LA: Louisiana State University Press, 1977.

Crozier, Alice C. *The Novels of Harriet Beecher Stowe*. New York: Oxford University Press, 1969.

Douglas, Ann. *The Feminization of American Culture*. New York: Alfred A. Knopf, Inc., 1977.

Fiedler, Leslie. *What Was Literature? Class Culture and Mass Society*. New York: Simon and Schuster, 1982.

Fields, Annie A., editor. *The Life and Letters of Harriet Beecher Stowe*. Boston: Houghton Mifflin Co., 1897.

Foster, Charles H. *The Rungless Ladder: Harriet Beecher Stowe and New England Puritanism*. Durham, NC: Duke University Press, 1954.

Gerson, Noel B. *Harriet Beecher Stowe*. New York: Praeger Publishers, Inc., 1976.

Jakoubek, Robert E. *Harriet Beecher Stowe*. New York: Chelsea House, 1989.

Johnston, Johanna. *Runaway to Heaven: The Story of Harriet Beecher Stowe*. New York: Doubleday & Co., Inc., 1963.

Kirkham, E. Bruce. *The Building of Uncle Tom's Cabin.* Knoxville, TN: University of Tennessee Press, 1977.

Lincoln, Abraham. *Speeches and Letters of Abraham Lincoln, 1832– 1865.* New York: E. P. Dutton & Co., 1907.

McCullough, David. "The Unexpected Mrs. Stowe," in *Brave Companions.* Englewood Cliffs, NJ: Prentice-Hall Press, 1992.

McFeely, William S. *Frederick Douglass.* New York: W. W. Norton & Co., 1991.

McPherson, James M. *Battle Cry of Freedom.* New York: Oxford University Press, Inc., 1988.

Northrup, Solomon. *Twelve Years A Slave;* edited by Sue Eakin and Joseph Logsdon. Baton Rouge: Louisiana State University Press, 1968.

Perry, Lewis and Michael Fellman, editors. *Antislavery Reconsidered: New Perspectives on the Abolitionists.* Baton Rouge: Louisiana State University Press, 1979.

Rourke, Constance Mayfield. *Trumpets of Jubilee: Henry Ward Beecher, Harriet Beecher Stowe, Lyman Beecher, Horace Greeley, P. T. Barnum.* New York: Harcourt, Brace & Co., 1927.

Stowe, Charles Edward, ed. *The Life of Harriet Beecher Stowe; Compiled from Her Letters and Journals.* Boston: Houghton Mifflin Co., 1889.

Stowe, Harriet Beecher. *A Key to Uncle Tom's Cabin.* Port Washington, NY: Kennikat Press, Inc., 1968. Facsimile of 1853 edition.

———. *Uncle Tom's Cabin or, Life Among the Lowly.* New York: Viking Penguin Inc., 1981.

———. *Works.* 16 volumes. Boston: Houghton Mifflin Company, 1916.

Stowe, Lyman Beecher. *Saints, Sinners and Beechers.* Indianapolis: The Bobbs-Merrill Company, 1934.

Ward, Geoffrey C. *The Civil War.* New York: Alfred A. Knopf, 1990.

Wilson, Edmund. "Harriet Beecher Stowe" and "Calvin Stowe" in *Patriotic Gore: Studies in the Literature of the American Civil War.* Boston: Northeastern University Press, 1984.

Wilson, Forrest. *Crusader in Crinoline: The Life of Harriet Beecher Stowe.* Philadelphia: J. B. Lippincott Co., 1941.

INDEX

ABOUT THE AUTHOR

Suzanne M. Coil worked in publishing for many years before becoming a full-time writer. Her books for young readers include *George Washington Carver*, *Poisonous Plants*, *The Poor in America*, and *Robert Hutchings Goddard*, among others. Ms. Coil is a member of the Authors Guild. She and her husband, Jesse, live in Covington, Lousiana.